WRITING
READABLE
SENTENCES

by Louis M. Kaiser

ISBN: 150276444X
ISBN 13: 9781502764447
Library of Congress Control Number: 2014918185
CreateSpace Independent Publishing Platform
North Charleston, South Carolina

CONTENTS

PREFACE

This handbook is intended to serve as a reference for anyone who is seeking to enhance his or her writing skills. There are two basic components of efficient written communication, defined in this handbook as getting your message across as quickly as possible without asking your reader to read between the lines. One component is the effective organization of the ideas and supporting information, which can go awry when there is not enough information, too much information, and/or misplaced information.1 The other component relates to the readability of individual sentences, the subject of this book. The readability of a sentence and its relevance to adjacent sentences decrease when there are words that do not fit with the rest of the sentence, too many or not enough words, and poorly located words.

In the sentence below, the reader is completely stymied. Is the sentence saying that trends in the retail industry, such as growth, have been one of the most accurate indicators of the strength or weakness of the American economy, or that the retail industry has been one of the strongest sectors of the American economy?

In recent decades, the retail industry has been one of the strongest indicators of American economic strength.

---

1 See *Analytic Writing Guide* (Kaiser and Pherson) for guidance on organizing the ideas and information in an analytic paper or report. The book also discusses the characteristics of well written topic sentences, the need to establish clear links between the topic sentence's analytic judgments and the supporting information, and the importance of brevity when writing for a busy reader.

Disconnects caused by the wrong words, too many or not enough words, and poorly located words can be a "show stopper" for the reader. Disconnects between words in adjacent sentences can have the same effect.

Sentences have to be clear as clear can be. The pace at which ideas and information is presented in written material is almost warp speed compared to the pace in verbal communication. Readers are expecting clarity. They do not want to have to pause and decipher unclear sentences in a memo or report. They may have a lot of other material to read. In addition, the reader does not have an opportunity to ask a question when confusion arises or elaboration is necessary. These demands place an incredibly high premium on readability.

SCOPE NOTE

The ideas and information in a readable sentence are conveyed accurately, completely, and quickly. This handbook identifies some three dozen guidelines for writing readable sentences that link well with surrounding sentences. The guidelines, which are grouped into six broad categories, address a set of common problems that emerged during a review of papers written by university students on a wide range of topics. These papers included grammatical errors to be sure—subject-verb agreement and the like—but other issues that were not related to grammar, such as an incomplete subject or a poor verb choice, much more often slowed me down or caused confusion and even complete bewilderment.

For each guideline, the handbook includes examples of problematic sentences taken from the student papers (with the problematic text in the sentence underlined in most cases), and the same sentences rewritten to address the problem. At the end of the book, there are exercises in applying the guidelines and "school solutions." Other revisions besides the "school solution" that address the writing problem and improve the sentence are equally valid. Almost all of the sentences in the exercises were excerpted from student papers.

The guidelines in this handbook are suggestions. Your objectives and the reader's needs are paramount and ultimately determine the final form of the writing. No one knows better than you what you are trying to accomplish and for whom you are writing. An e-mail from one doctor to another about a patient's condition would look much different than an e-mail to a patient about his or her condition. The same e-mail to a patient would look much different if the doctor was trying to reassure the patient about his or her condition.

The handbook is intended to be used with other published materials and your own thoughts on writing readable sentences. If you are seeking to write as clearly as possible, these guidelines will help. Even good writers, who possess the skill to attempt more complex, longer sentences, will occasionally write an unreadable sentence. The best way to learn the guidelines and make them second nature is to apply them over and over again. The exercises at the end of the book are intended to begin that process. The more you work at making your sentences as readable as possible, the easier it will become. Along the way you will discover new guidelines for writing readable sentences and expand upon the ones already in this handbook. Several blank "Notes" pages are included at the end of this handbook for recording your own thoughts and ideas.

ACKNOWLEDGEMENTS

First and foremost, I have to thank all those who were brave enough to give me samples of their writing that I could review to obtain material for this handbook. I simply could not have written this book without their cooperation. Allowing someone to scour and critique your writing is not easy. Most of us are not willing to expose ourselves to this kind of scrutiny, especially when there is no requirement to do so. I would be remiss if I did not also thank Dennis Bowden, who reviewed the manuscript and provided valuable suggestions related to both content and organization.

EACH SENTENCE IS A DISCRETE SYSTEM AND AN ELEMENT IN A BROADER SYSTEM

Having to slog through a sentence that is poorly written is not fun. How long do you think a reader will continue to read if he or she has to decipher every sentence to make sense out of it? Probably not long. At some point, the reader concludes that the writing is not going to improve and stops reading. A sentence can fail to convey what the author intended to convey when only a part of the sentence fails. The sentence at best takes the reader longer to comprehend and at worst may convey almost nothing.

I am confident that the author of any confusing sentence, if asked what he or she meant, could clarify most of the time. Think of each sentence as a discrete system. Take the time to carefully review this system and write what you mean. Every word in the sentence has a role to play in conveying the intended thought. Do not just assume the sentence is readable. Assuming the opposite stance—i.e. that the sentence is problematic—is a better approach. Every first draft usually has a lot of problematic sentences. The readability of a sentence can diminish because of problems with content (missing and inaccurate ideas and information) and problems with form (syntax and structure). As a general rule, fix the content problems first, then the problems with form.

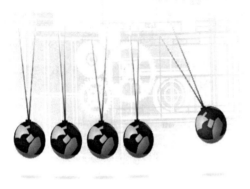

Every sentence in every paragraph and every paragraph in every paper should have a main point irrespective of the type of paper. Every sentence should have a main point related to what you are trying to accomplish at that point in the paragraph. If the paragraph lacks a main point and an objective, anything and everything is eligible for being the sentence's main point. A sentence cannot have a main point in isolation from from the main point and objective of the paragraph.

Each sentence in a paper is part of a broader system that is the paper or report in its entirety. When one sentence succeeds in conveying exactly what you intended the sentence to convey, it sets up the next sentence to also succeed. Conversely, when one sentence fails, a chain reaction occurs that lowers the readability of follow-on sentences. (See Appendix.) Each sentence has a role in conveying the paragraph's message. If enough individual sentences fail, the paragraph fails, and if enough paragraphs fail, the paper fails. The reader has little idea what the author's broader message is. A typical response from readers in this situation is, "I have no idea what I just read."

FIRST THINGS FIRST:
PAY CLOSE ATTENTION TO
THE SUBJECT AND VERB

The two most important components of every sentence are the subject and the verb. If either one is problematic, the sentence will fail to communicate the intended message even if everything else in the sentence is written well. The sentence's subject and verb should focus on the main point of the sentence and be as sharply defined and easy to understand as possible. The verb should complement the subject and the rest of the sentence, or the reader is almost immediately confused. Sometimes, the subject needs to be expanded to fit properly with the rest of the sentence. The subject of the sentence cannot just half fit.

Focus the Sentence's Subject and Verb on the Main Point. Build the sentence around a subject and verb that address this main idea. When reviewing *each and every sentence,* ask yourself "is this the right subject" and "is this the best verb" for what you are trying to convey at that point in the paragraph and paper. This focus will help to establish a connection with previous sentences and to keep follow-on sentences fixed on the paragraph's main point.

What is the main idea that you are seeking to convey? A sentence must have a main point before you can select a subject and verb to address a main point. Identifying a main point is not a given. It requires some thought.

A problematic subject can significantly skew the sentence's main point. In the example below, *majority* is a poor subject because the main idea in the sentence is about the views of the majority and not the majority per se. The two sentences convey somewhat different ideas. The first sentence allows for the possibility that the majority also has crazy and dangerous ideas but not so in the second sentence.

Although Montesquieu argued that ministers should execute the people's wishes, the <u>majority</u> must have coherent and helpful ideas for this to be accomplished. **Better**: Although Montesquieu argued that ministers should execute the people's wishes, the views of the majority must be coherent and helpful for this to be accomplished.

Inadequate emphasis on a sentence's main point can occur in a variety of sentence constructions. The main point of the sentence almost always should be placed in an independent clause.

An **independent clause** is a clause that can <u>stand alone</u> as a sentence and <u>expresses a complete thought.</u>

Note: in the examples below, assume the paragraph's focus is on Napoleon's power at its peak and not on his humble beginnings. The remainder of the paragraph would discuss Napoleon's political influence, countries that he had subjugated through war or diplomacy, etc.

Inadequate emphasis on main point: Napoleon was born in a small town in Corsica in 1769, and he became the most powerful man in Europe after a series of stunning military victories. (Main point is in an independent clause, but so is the secondary information, which is getting "equal billing," i.e. emphasis.)

Napoleon, who became the most powerful man in Europe after a series of stunning military victories, was born in a small town in Corsica in 1769. (Main point is in a dependent clause.)

Napoleon, the most powerful man in Europe after a series of stunning military victories, was born in a small town in Corsica in 1769. (Main point is in an adjective phrase.)

Better: Napoleon, who was born in a small town in Corsica in 1769, became the most powerful man in Europe after a series of stunning military victories. His influence extended …

Secondary information, which often is quite important to fully understanding the main point, elaborates on both actors and actions and can be descriptive or explanatory. Descriptive information typically elaborates on the actor, while explanatory information elaborates on the context of the action. Secondary information is typically placed in phrases and dependent clauses, including adverb clauses.

Descriptive information: Julius Caesar, *who was born around ...*

Explanatory information: *Consumed with ambition,* Julius Caesar played a major role in the demise of the Roman Republic.

Dependent clauses can modify the subject or the verb and are great for inserting descriptive and explanatory information into a sentence. Nero, *who was the son of the sister of Emperor Caligula,* brutally persecuted Christians. **Adverb clauses** are great for highlighting differences and providing important context: *After seeing Rome burn,* Nero slept like a baby.

Emphasis on secondary information, whatever the type, makes the main point harder to discern. The resulting sentence is sometimes wordy and convoluted.

This revelation corroborates an earlier report by CNN quoting a Kenyan official as saying that the stockpile of weapons in the rented store might explain why the terrorists held out for four days without running out of ammunition. **Better:** This revelation corroborates a Kenyan official's claim—cited in a CNN report—that the stockpile of weapons in the rented store might explain why the terrorists held out for four days without running out of ammunition. The terrorists ...

The main point of a sentence that includes the rationale or motive for taking some action can change depending on what time frame the sentence is emphasizing. When emphasizing the immediate action, the rationale is just as important. When emphasizing the long term consequences of the action, the rationale for taking the action becomes secondary information.

> Last year the company was concerned about its huge debt and fundamentally changed its operating standards.

> Concerned about its huge debt, the company in 1990 fundamentally changed its operating standards and maintained that same business model for more than 20 years.

A sentence in which the main point is implied is a sentence that lacks a strong subject and verb. Is there a noun in the sentence that could serve as a strong subject and allow for a more direct sentence? Once a better subject is identified, an appropriate verb to complement the subject almost always will emerge. Sentences that begin with "another method" or "another goal" or something similar can also be rewritten with a stronger subject and verb that conveys the main idea more directly and effectively. The main idea in these sentences is sometimes buried in prepositional phrases and *that* clauses. Find the strong subject and verb, and insert *also* into the sentence as a substitute for *another whatever*.

> A cyber-attack of any significant caliber <u>is too sophisticated</u> for most Jihadist hackers today. **Better:** Most Jihadist hackers today lack the technical ability to conduct a cyber-attack of any significant caliber.

> <u>Another method</u> that hackers use to gather your personal information is known as key-logging, which monitors and records the keystrokes used to access a file. **Better:** Hackers also use key logging, which monitors and records the keystrokes used to access a file, to obtain your personal information.

<u>A prominent difficulty</u> in the acceptance of Western-style democracy in Asia was the region's disparate sociocultural and religious norms. **Better**: The region's disparate sociocultural and religious norms greatly hindered the acceptance of Western-style democracy in Asia.

If a "to be" verb is the main verb in the sentence, look for a potentially stronger subject and verb. Look for a "to-be" verb that can be deleted in sentences in which the "to-be" verb is followed by an adjective. A strong verb may exist that will more directly convey the main point of the sentence. Another place to look for a gratuitous "to-be" verb is in sentences in which the subject of the sentence involves motive, intent, or objective. Also, is there an entity in the sentence that is taking or took some action but is not the subject? If there is, perhaps it should be the subject. If some entity's statement is the main point of the sentence, is that entity the subject of the sentence? Maybe it should be as well.

Format, word choice, and narration are influential on the novel's final form. **Better**: Format, word choice, and narration influence the novel's final form.

The prime minister's objective was to create a diplomatic crisis that would require international mediation. **Better**: The prime minister aimed to create a diplomatic crisis that would require international mediation.

The attack according to the group was in retaliation for Kenya's military intervention in Somalia. **Better**: The group claimed the attack was in retaliation for Kenya's military intervention in Somalia.

Opt for the Most Straightforward Subject and the Most Direct Verb.
Subjects and verbs that digress obscure the sentence's main point.

Look for subjects that appear wordier and more complex than necessary. Ask yourself what is another, more readable way of saying the same thing. Keep it simple if you can. If the sentence's verb appears to be taking a winding path to the sentence's main point by emphasizing an auxiliary or intermediate aspect of the main point, a shorter, more direct verb probably is needed.

Cities in Greece usually quarried the closest white marbles because the <u>economic status</u> of most cities could not <u>support constant funding for</u> extensive quarrying in more remote locations. **Better**: Most cities in Greece usually quarried the closest white marbles because their economies could not afford extensive quarrying in more remote locations.

With the conquests of Alexander the Great, Greece <u>began the trend</u> of transporting marble from incredibly large distances. **Better**: With the conquests of Alexander the Great, Greece began transporting marble from incredibly large distances.

The Diem government <u>went as far as banning</u> ... **Better**: The Diem government banned ... *Unless a spectrum of possibilities is apparent and important to the reader, the phrase "went as far as" does not add very much. In addition, some might argue that Diem did far worse and the phrase is not accurate.*

A passive voice construction, where the subject is the receiver of the action rather than the doer of the action, works in some sentences, especially those in which the doer is not known, or the focus of the sentence is on the result and the doer is understood. (See examples below.) Passive voice constructions are also used in scientific writing where the researcher is often the actor and sentences of the type "I then put the material in a test tube" would put the focus on the researcher and not the research. Generally speaking, active voice is better than passive voice.

I was robbed twice in my two summer visits to Rome.

All of the homes on our street and a neighboring street were damaged.

If a passive-voice sentence contains only one main idea, the sentence construction may not be optimal, but the main idea is generally readable. A passive voice construction in the first part of a sentence, however, can lock you into using another passive voice construction or making a confusing reference if a second main idea follows. The subject of the second main idea in the sentence is not immediately apparent. The best way to fix the sentence is to use the active voice.

Musique concrète was developed in 1948 by a French composer named Pierre Schaeffer, and <u>was inspired by his experience</u> in radio as well as film soundtracks. **Better:** A French composer named Pierre Schaeffer, inspired by his experience in radio as well as film soundtracks, developed *musique concrete* in 1948.

During the previous year, Henry Kissinger had been tasked by Nixon to "probe the possibility of resuming relations with China," which prompted the former to prepare policy options toward China. **Better**: Henry Kissinger prepared policy options toward China after a tasking from Nixon the previous year to "probe the possibility of resuming relations with China."

Select a Verb that Is In Sync with the Entire Sentence. Not surprisingly, a verb that does not fit well with the subject and all the other parts of the sentence reduces the sentence's readability. A poor verb choice can create a sentence that is almost incomprehensible. If the verb is acting on more than one object, make sure it fits with all of them. Do not accept a verb that is almost in sync with the subject and the rest of the sentence. If you suspect the verb does not fit in the sentence, substitute another verb that is a synonym. If the disconnect remains or seems to have grown, a much different verb needs to be found.

> Somalia's weak central authority <u>makes</u> its long coastline a staging area for international piracy and attacks on US-flagged vessels. Somalia's weak central authority <u>creates</u> *(ugh!)* its long coastline a staging area for international piracy and attacks on US-flagged vessels. *The sentence, because of the poor verb choice, reads as if the "central authority" is doing this on purpose.* **Better**: Somalia's weak central authority enables its long coastline to be used as a staging area for international piracy and attacks on US-flagged vessels. *The subject in this sentence also is problematic. What is doing the enabling: the weak central authority or the weakness of the central authority? Fixing one part of a problematic sentence often exposes another problem in the sentence.*

> Through different wars and upheavals, freedom in America finally <u>reached</u> what we know it as today. **Better**: Through different wars and upheavals, freedom in America finally evolved into what we know it as today.

> The picture of the Buddhist monk on fire <u>brings</u> a contrast of light and dark that represents good and evil. **Better**: The picture of the Buddhist monk on fire creates a contrast of light and dark that represents good and evil.

The verb may fit well with the first few words after the verb and then utterly fail.

> India and Singapore are <u>providing</u> technology and manufacturing capabilities that may soon rival Japan's capabilities. **Better:** India and Singapore are developing technology and manufacturing capabilities that may soon rival Japan's capabilities.

"Providing" as a verb does not make much sense without someone receiving whatever is being provided.

Sparingly Use *Result* as a Subject

Unless you are documenting a science experiment, using *result* as a subject can create a cumbersome sentence. Sometimes, deleting *result* and inserting *when* or *after* is all that is needed to create a more direct sentence. The result or consequence is implied by the sequence of events as described in the sentence.

The result of the massive industrialization that occurred during World War II was that America became an economic super power. **Better:** After the massive industrialization that occurred during World War II, America became an economic super power.

The end result of a completed sticker chart was to allow students to pick an item from a prize box. **Better:** After completing their sticker chart, students were allowed to pick an item from a prize box.

Complete the Subject. Writers, cognizant of what they are trying to convey, may read more into the subject of the sentence than what is actually there on paper. The resulting sentence is not readable because a critical part of the main idea, the subject, is not complete. The subject in these sentences is often a single noun that needs expansion or elaboration. Look for subjects that are not modified by an adjective, phrase, or clause and assess whether the subject needs to be expanded.

With the spread of colonization, restraints worked their way into the New World. **Better:** With the spread of colonization, restraints on freedom and personal liberty worked their way into the New World.

12

Hawaii is more tolerant of different cultures than other any state because ... **Better:** Residents of Hawaii are more tolerant of different cultures than residents of other states because ...

Freedom in America reflects the history of America's social, political, and societal development. **Better:** The quest for freedom in America reflects the history of America's social, political, and societal development.

Any subject, including those that already are being extensively modified, may need expansion.

Chinese military and nuclear defenses were suddenly and quickly escalated during the 1960s in an effort to match the military capabilities of the US and the USSR. **Better**: Spending on Chinese military and nuclear defenses was suddenly and quickly escalated during the 1960s in an effort to match the military capabilities of the US and USSR. *Is "spending" the optimum subject for this sentence? What about making "China" the subject?*

A subject and verb that address the same concept is a sure tip off of a serious glitch with either the subject or the verb. In many of these sentences, the subject is incomplete and poorly defined.

The origins of the horror of Thich Quang Duc's self-immolation began in 1955. **Better**: The events that led to the horror of Thich Quang Duc's self-immolation began in 1955.

The end of the Washington Naval Conference did not end the tension ... **Better**: The Washington Naval Treaty and other agreements, which were negotiated at the Washington Naval Conference, did not end ...

CONSTRUCT GRASPABLE SENTENCES THAT UNITE AND ADVANCE THE MESSAGE

Information in a graspable sentence is readily understandable and allows the reader to move on to the next sentence fully prepared to understand the next sentence. A graspable sentence does not inundate the reader with too much information that appears unrelated or moves in too many different conceptual directions. When the period comes at the end of the sentence, the reader does not feel like he or she needs to reread the sentence or take two aspirin. At the same time, the sentence contains enough content and substance for the reader to grasp a complete idea. The reader does not feel as if something important is missing. A graspable sentence also is direct and gets to the main point as quickly as possible. It does not take the reader on a roundabout journey. A graspable sentence also links to previous ideas and information and moves forward in a steady progression that advances the reader's knowledge and understanding.

Use Two Sentences to Enhance Readability. The length of a sentence should not be the deciding factor in opting to break up the sentence. More important than length is the readability of the sentence. Readability diminishes when the structure of the sentence does not allow the writer to fully establish and explain the connection between different elements in the sentence. These sentences often begin with a key idea and end with an explanation that only tangentially addresses this key idea. The sentence does not deliver, and a second sentence is needed.

The foundation for Chicago's incredible growth has its roots in the fortunate circumstances in which Chicago found itself during the mid-1800s as it established itself as a geographical and commercial center for the rapidly expanding western frontier. *What were the "fortunate circumstances"?* **Better**: The foundation for Chicago's incredible growth has its roots in the fortunate circumstances in which Chicago found itself during the mid-1800s. Chicago was uniquely positioned geographically and commercially to benefit from the rapid westward expansion of America's frontier.

Readability also diminishes when a sentence shifts conceptual directions too much and creates a pin-ball-like effect on the reader. A good rule of thumb is to break up a sentence that shifts focus or direction more than once. The focus of a sentence typically shifts when a new subject and new verb—i.e. a new idea—is introduced in an independent clause. Shifts in focus also occur when the sentence contains clauses led by "although," "despite," and similar words that suggest a contradiction or complication.

Sentences that shift focus more than once are more difficult to process and are conceptually complicated as they bounce from one idea to another. Readers may forget some of the content in the first part of the sentence as they focus on understanding the second half.

Although numerous organizations measure corruption using a variety of metrics, all three of the statistical studies noted previously use the CPI, and Christoph Stefes asserts that the CPI remains the "most prominent empirical study" of corruption despite the difficulty of accurately measuring a phenomenon that is often hidden. **Better**: Although numerous organizations measure corruption using a variety of metrics, all three of the statistical studies noted previously use the CPI. Christoph Stefes asserts that the CPI remains the "most prominent empirical study" of corruption despite the difficulty of accurately measuring a phenomenon that is often hidden.

Reports to corporate executives should include a discussion of all the factors needed to make a good business decision, or the risk of a bad investment is high, and such reports also should be concise but provide enough detail to be convincing. **Better**: Reports to corporate executives should include a discussion of all the factors needed to make a good business decision, or the risk of a bad investment is high. Such papers should be concise but provide enough detail to be convincing.

A clause or phrase works best if it is adjacent to the noun it is modifying, but this arrangement is not always possible. An alternative to moving the clause closer to the noun is to write a new sentence, particularly if the clause has a much different focus than the main point in the sentence. In the first example below, the focus of the sentence is on the marble's popularity while the clause focuses on transporting the marble. The sentence is grammatically correct, but its readability can be improved. Putting the information in a separate sentence also highlights its importance.

East Greek white marbles became popular in the third century AD, especially the large-grained varieties from the Rhodope massif found on the islands of Prokonnesos and Thasos, which were easily extracted and transported by sea. **Better:** East Greek white marbles became popular in the third century AD, especially the large-grained varieties from the Rhodope massif found on the islands of Prokonnesos and Thasos. These marbles were easily extracted and transported by sea.

As an adult, Shaarawi wrote about her activities outside the home and helped to organize lectures for women that were given by a European traveler, which eventually led to Egyptian women also speaking out and giving lectures. **Better**: As an adult, Shaarawi wrote about her activities outside the home and helped to organize lectures for women that were given by a European traveler. These lectures prompted Egyptian women to speak out and give lectures themselves.

Make the Idea Easy for the Reader to Process. Is the main idea readily apparent from the words that are in the sentence? If the sentence contains more than one main idea, as in a compound sentence, review each idea separately. If one of the main ideas is clear, you may read over and miss the idea that is not.

When you review a sentence, ask yourself what was the main idea you just read. If the words you articulated out loud are slightly different than the words you read, the sentence probably needs fine tuning. If the words you articulated out loud bear little or no resemblance to the words you read, a major rewrite of the main idea probably is needed. If you are trying to gain style points by maintaining some kind of parallel structure in the sentence and the words are not clear, forget the style points.

The tactic of terrorism may never change, but the reasons motivating the terrorist will. **Better:** Terrorism will always exist, but the reasons motivating the terrorist will change. **Or:** The objective of terrorism, to scare and intimidate, may never change … **Or:** The tactics of terrorism, which rely on destruction and violence, …

With the coming of new states into the Union, the question of slavery controlled politics in America up to the Civil War. **Better:** With the coming of new states into the Union, the question of slavery became the dominant political issue in America up to the Civil War.

A compound sentence has two independent clauses joined by a conjunction such as *and* or *but.*

Include all the information that the reader needs to quickly process the main idea in the sentence. Think of the main idea in the sentence as made up of different parts, much like a math equation, where A+B=C. If B is missing or is poorly stated, the reader will not be able to understand how A=C. In the example below, the insertion of key information that was missing into the original sentence substantially changed the sentence and required a major revision. Making the sentence more readable often is an iterative process when new information is added.

> Most politically-motivated terrorism is over territorial gains for a population that is marginally represented within a country. *What is meant by "territorial gains"?* **First iteration**: Most politically-motivated terrorism occurs when a population is marginally represented in a country and perceives itself unable to obtain an equitable distribution of the land and its resources. **Second iteration**: Populations that are marginally represented in a country and perceive themselves unable to obtain an equitable distribution of the land and its resources account for most politically-motivated terrorism.

Indicators that you may have over complicated the sentence include: a subject represented by a noun phrase that seems to go on forever (first example below); text that discusses a simple idea using unnecessarily complex concepts (first, second, and third examples); the inclusion of nonessential facts and details (second example); and, perhaps the best indicator, a perception that the main idea is anything but simply stated (all four). You can make the sentence easier for the reader to process by simplifying the sentence construction, using simple and direct language, and deleting information that is not central to the main point.

Leveraging the company's history of successfully developing new weapons while simultaneously improving the capabilities of

<u>older systems</u> creates <u>a high growth environment</u> for continued arms contracts going forward. **Better**: The company's proven ability to develop new weapons and improve the capabilities of older systems suggests the company will continue to win new arms contracts.

Historians concerned with changes in economic and political <u>theatres</u> ... **Better**: Historians concerned with economic and political changes ...

Even though the lack of government regulation of commercial banks' involvement in stock market investment <u>led to over-zealous bank investment in securities</u> that contributed to the Great Depression, the Glass-Steagall Act of 1933, which limited such investment, faced serious political opposition. **Better:** Even though the lack of government regulation of commercial bank's involvement in stock market investment contributed greatly to the Great Depression, the Glass-Steagall Act of 1933, which limited such investment, faced serious political opposition.

Both Stevie and Winnie try to assume roles that are exceptions to the typical gender behavior in the novel, but they are ultimately unable to operate away from their <u>expected functions</u>. **Better**: Both Stevie and Winnie try to assume roles that are exceptions to the typical gender behavior in this novel, but they were unable to do so.

A single word can overcomplicate a sentence and stymie the reader if the reader is not familiar with the word and the concept is key to understanding the sentence's main idea. Abstract, out-of-the-blue concepts are almost impossible for the reader to process.

The main tenets of Confucianism, which are ingrained in Asian political thinking, are <u>incommensurate</u> to Western ideals. **Better**: The main tenets of Confucianism, which are ingrained in Asian political thinking, are not the same as Western ideals.

The Great Leap Forward and Cultural Revolution had exhausted China of its resources, and new <u>reparative</u> initiatives required resources that were not available in China. **Better**: The Great Leap Forward and Cultural Revolution had exhausted China of its resources, and new initiatives to rebuild China required resources that were not available in China.

Although the idea of <u>voluntarism</u> was present in the formation of the Taiwanese and South Korean democracies, ... **Better**: Although most of the population in Taiwan and South Korea supported the formation of democracy, ... *What was meant by "voluntarism" became apparent in the paper two paragraphs later. The adage "better late than never" does not apply to writing.*

Make sure that information that is introduced to define an element in the sentence is clearly linked to that element and is not read as a separate part of the sentence. The potential for the reader to misconstrue this information increases when a comma is used to separate an introductory infinitive phrase from an extensive amount of definitional information. The reader finds what looks like the sentence's subject, then starts to look for a verb, does not find one, and becomes totally confused and forced to reread the sentence. Finally, the reader gets it. A number of options are available to improve the sentence's readability.

To ensure that a belief is correct, <u>an exact reflection of a happening in the external world instead of a misinterpretation or deception of input</u>, proper justification is necessary. **Better**: To ensure that a belief is correct—an exact reflection of a happening in the external world instead of a misinterpretation or deception of input—proper justification is necessary. *Use em dashes rather commas.* **Or:** To ensure that a belief is correct, i.e. an exact reflection of a happening in the external world instead of a misinterpretation or deception of input, ... **Or:** To ensure that a belief is correct and an exact reflection of a happening in the external world instead of a misinterpretation or deception of input, ...

Long—and even short—introductory phrases and clauses can create a cumbersome and less readable sentence if they disrupt the connection between the different elements of the main idea. Processing the significance of a large amount of introductory information is difficult without a subject and verb that provides a basis and context for understanding its relevance. Minimize the amount of introductory information and get to the subject as quickly as possible to provide that context. In some cases, the ideas in these phrases and clauses are the main point and need to be worked more directly into the sentence. The resulting sentence is shorter and snappier. Ask yourself whether you can write the sentence without the introductory clause or phrase.

So effective and high-functioning has the US constitutional model been that since its inauguration in the 18th century, many other nations have borrowed from its democratic principles. **Better:** Since the Constitution's inauguration in the 18th century, many other nations have borrowed from its democratic principles because the US constitutional model has been so effective and high-functioning.

Although it would take three wars with Prussia's neighbors during a seven year period, Otto von Bismarck succeeded in forging a unified Germany. **Better:** Otto von Bismarck exploited three wars with Prussia's neighbors during a seven-year period to forge a unified Germany.

> <u>So with this knowledge and insight</u>, we gain an understanding of why this event was so important. **Better**: This knowledge and insight helps us to understand why this event was so important.

A series of "that" clauses in a sentence is sometimes difficult for the reader to follow even when they are all clearly written. Review the sentence to determine whether all of these clauses are necessary. In some cases, an entire clause may be redundant and can be deleted or turned into a short phrase attached to the preceding clause. Sometimes, a *that* clause needs to be changed to a nonrestrictive *which* clause to deemphasize the importance of the information and reduce the reader's sense of information overload. If a sentence seems like it contains too many *that* clauses, it probably does.

> I recommended that teachers provide independent work that the special education students could work on until they are able to begin their instruction of the students that usually takes an hour to complete. **Better:** I recommended that teachers provide independent work for the special education students until the teachers are able to begin their instruction, which usually takes an hour to complete.

Nonrestrictive clauses by definition do not provide information that is important to fully understanding the main point of the sentence. They are set off by commas.

If you have a long clause or phrase that you stumble over when you read it, ask yourself whether the clause or phrase can be written more clearly and succinctly. Is there a simple idea behind all those words?

The different instrumental effects struggle for recognition and prominence in the recording, hinting at contemporaneous real world activism and revolt without the use of <u>explicit references to the song's subject matter lyrically</u>. **Better:** The different instrumental effects struggle for recognition and prominence in the recording, hinting at contemporaneous real world activism and revolt without the use of lyrics.

At the beginning of World War II, President Roosevelt authorized the funding of nuclear fission research out of concern that Nazi Germany was <u>conducting similar research that was intended to create the basis for an atomic bomb</u>. **Better:** At the beginning of World War II, President Roosevelt authorized the funding of nuclear fission research out of concern that Nazi Germany was seeking to develop an atomic bomb.

If the sentence contains a long source-attribution phrase, begin the sentence with the main idea and end the sentence with the source-attribution phrase. Most of the time, the main point is more important than the sourcing information. The reader may end up reading two lines of text before getting to the main point. The sentence can momentarily seem like gobbledygook that has no point.

According to the director of the Center for African Security, Strategic and International Studies, a research think tank linked to the Ugandan military, and several media reports produced by investigative journalists, Al Shabaab's network of legal and illicit business activities is extensive. **Better:** Al Shabaab's network of legal and illicit business activities is extensive, according to the director of the Center for African Security, Strategic and International Studies, a research think tank linked to the Ugandan military, and several media reports produced by investigative journalists.

Rework Sentences That End Too Abruptly. A sentence that ends too abruptly often reads like an unsupported assertion. When reviewing your sentences, look for short sentences that immediately raise major questions but fail to answer them. Often the explanation is in the next sentence, and just as often, the two sentences can be combined. Do not leave the reader with a sense that something is missing. Combining the sentences strengthens the linkage between the two ideas and sometimes eliminates an intermediate concept that is serving as the subject of the second sentence. This intermediate concept is often an abstraction that is less readable than a more tangible subject.

Special education teachers need to be aware of all the legal mandates, ethical standards, and assessment strategies. This awareness must be applied in making sound eligibility, placement, and program decisions. **Better:** Special education teachers need to be aware of all the legal mandates, ethical standards, and assessment strategies to make sound eligibility, placement, and program decisions.

Involvement in community activities is vitally important to educators. Educators need to establish a personal connection with their students and their families. **Better:** Involvement in community activities is vitally important to educators because it helps them establish a personal connection with their students and their families.

Maximize the Value Added. Provide as much content as possible. Avoid gratuitous declarations that something is apparent or evident. Rather than announce that a similarity or difference is apparent, just state the similarity or difference and, if possible, elaborate. The resulting sentence will be more direct and will read less like everyone should know this and more like an insight or a conclusion, which it is. Moreover, when these gratuitous declarations are eliminated, the connection between the different elements of a main idea is strengthened, and a more direct sentence is created, as in the second example below. To convey uncertainty, use "appear" or "apparently are" as the verb.

> The difference between humans and machines in free will is apparent. Humans can make choices and decisions. **Better**: Humans, unlike machines, have the free will to make choices and decisions.

> In wake of the Al-Shabaab attacks in Kenya and Uganda, it is evident that Al-Shabaab is willing to attack outside of Somalia. **Better**: The Al-Shabaab attacks in Kenya and Uganda demonstrate that Al-Shabaab is willing to attack outside of Somalia.

> The similarities between the poem's moral warnings about greed and some teachings in the Bible are apparent. **Better:** The poem's moral warnings about greed are similar to some teachings in the Bible. **Or:** The poem's moral warnings about greed appear similar to some teachings in the Bible.

Provide more value-added than just announcing a development has had an impact or effect. When used as a verb, *impact* often tells the reader nothing. Be explicit. Tell the reader what the impact was. *Affect* is another verb that should be used carefully for the same reason: it can mean anything. Sentences using *impact* and *effect* as subjects provide more information to the reader, but more direct and readable sentence constructions are available. Find the infinitive that usually follows later in the sentence and build a sentence around a strong verb using this infinitive. The *impact* or *effect* is implicit in this verb. Follow-on sentences that use *impact* and *effect* as subjects are clear once the impact or effect has been identified.

Justice Breyer cited examples from the kitchen appliance industry to show how allowing manufacturers to set minimum prices affected consumer prices. **Better:** Justice Breyer cited examples from the kitchen appliance industry to show how allowing manufacturers to set minimum prices increased consumer prices.

The impact of the steam engine was to allow factories to be built where water power was unavailable. **Better:** The steam engine allowed factories to be built where water power was unavailable.

Clean Up Roundabout Sentences. The repetition in a roundabout sentence requires readers to process unnecessary information and can sometimes leave readers totally baffled. Sometimes, the sentence eventually gets to a main point, and sometimes, it ends where it started. In some roundabout sentences, a better subject may be buried somewhere in the middle of the sentence, and the sentence needs to be reconstructed around this better subject.

In the first example below, "use of computer technology" and "provides teachers with a means" are similar ideas. The sentence in the second example has a more serious problem in that the sentence has made a complete circle, and as a result, a major point is not at all explained. The sentence went nowhere. In the third example, the repetition occurs when the term cited in the first part of the sentence is defined at the very end of the sentence.

Use of computer technology provides special education teachers with a means to reinforce skills that their students are learning in the classroom. **Better:** Special education teachers can use computer technology to reinforce skills that their students are learning in the classroom.

The male characters are completely self-absorbed, and any act of kindness by them that seems to contradict this can be explained by the characters' selfishness. **Better:** The male characters are completely self-absorbed, and any act of kindness by them that seems to contradict this can be explained as a ruse intended to achieve selfish goals.

The Beatles' use of *musique concrète* made the colorful, eye-opening world of an LSD trip accessible to non-drug-users by using real world sounds and manual manipulations of sounds. **Better:** The Beatles' use of *musique concrete*—real world sounds and the manual manipulations of sounds—made the colorful, eye-opening world of an LSD trip accessible to non-drug-users.

Optimize the Flow of Information between Sentences. The flow of information between sentences comes to a screeching halt when one sentence says one thing, and the next sentence appears to contradict it. Somewhere in one of the sentences, there is either an error that needs correcting or a major discrepancy that needs explaining.

Two teams tied for a division must play a tie-breaking game even if both teams have already qualified for the postseason. The team losing the tie-breaking game qualifies for a wildcard berth only if its regular-season record is among the league's two best records for non-division winners. *One team appears to win a playoff berth in the first sentence only to have it taken back in the second sentence. What gives???*

The connection between the main ideas in back-to-back sentences should be immediately clear. The two sentences should appear relevant to one another. Establishing a missing link between back-to-back sentences sometimes requires replacing several words and sometimes just the insertion of a single word. The absence of a connection between sentences is not as big a problem as when the sentences appear to take contradictory positions, but it is close. The reader will feel momentarily lost.

The church not only lets light bleed through it but also absorbs light through its sustainable materials. The concrete shells are covered with a patented, self-cleaning mixture of photo catalytic particles that oxidize pollutants when exposed to sunlight. *What is the connection between the two sentences?* **Better:** The church not only lets light bleed through it, but also uses light to help maintain its beauty. The concrete shells are covered with a patented, self-cleaning mixture of photo catalytic particles that oxidize pollutants when exposed to sunlight.

Meier uniquely portrays the traditional elements often found in a church. While most churches depict the "Holy Trinity" through sculpture and interior artwork, the Jubilee church uses three large curving "sails" that enclose the church nave. *The connection between "traditional elements" and the "Holy Trinity" is a little tenuous.* **Better**: Meier uniquely portrays the traditional religious elements often found in a church. While most churches depict the "Holy Trinity" through sculpture and interior artwork, the Jubilee church uses three large curving "sails" that enclose the church nave.

Before the Europeans inhabited North America, native Americans had unlimited freedom. Where we started, however, is actually closest to where we ended up. The origins of freedom in North America were very peculiar. *The main idea in the third sentence does not appear relevant to the main idea in the first two sentences. A more relevant subject is needed in the third sentence.* **Better**: The path to freedom in North America was not a linear progression.

The progression of ideas between sentences is improved when the preceding sentence ends with an idea that sets up the main idea in the next sentence. Rearrange information in sentences and move sentences to maintain better continuity between sentences. Improving the flow of ideas between sentences helps the reader to follow the bigger story that is being told. A separate sentence that includes primarily background information, as in the third example below, can disrupt the flow of ideas. This material belongs in a dependent clause.

The Fair Labor Act of 1938 forever changed regulations governing the retail industry by banning child labor and limiting the maximum workweek to 44 hours. Over the next 50 years, a number of legislative acts can be traced to the Fair Labor Act, including ... The Fair Labor Act also required "time-and-a-half" overtime for certain jobs. **Better:** The Fair Labor Act of 1938 required "time-and-a-half" overtime for certain jobs, banned child labor, and limited the maximum workweek to 44 hours. The Act forever changed regulations governing the retail industry. Over the next 50 years, a number of legislative acts can be traced to the Fair Labor Act, including ...

Two American citizens, Ali Yasin Ahmed and Mohamed Yusef, were apprehended last year in Africa en route to Yemen. These individuals had trained with the terrorist organization Al-Shabaab and participated in its terrorist operations. Police apprehended the two Americans after noting discrepancies in their documentation and nervous behavior. **Better:** Two American citizens, Ali Yasin Ahmed and Mohamed Yusef, who had trained with the terrorist organization Al-Shabaab and participated in its operations, were apprehended last year in Africa en route to Yemen. Police apprehended the two Americans after noting discrepancies in their documentation and nervous behavior.

King called for a nonviolent campaign to end racial segregation and economic injustice. In April 1964, he was arrested for parading without a permit. Eight pastors wrote and published a newspaper article titled "A Call for Unity," in which they criticized King and his methods. **Better**: King called for a nonviolent campaign to end racial segregation and economic injustice. After he was arrested for parading without a permit in April 1964, eight white pastors from Alabama wrote and published a newspaper article entitled "A Call for Unity" in which they criticized King and his methods.

Consider moving up information in clauses that are led by *as* and *because* if the clauses only provide definitional-like elaboration or information that is well known. These clauses create sentences that move backwards rather than forward. Putting the explanation or information in a "which" clause after the subject is a simple fix. Save the "because" clause for sentences in which the information is not so well known.

Tomorrow Never Knows was a vast departure from the typical Beatles sound as it used *musique concrète* to create an ethereal, LSD-inspired soundscape. **Better:** *Tomorrow Never Knows*, which used *musique concrète* to create an ethereal, LSD-inspired soundscape, was a vast departure from the typical Beatles sound.

The hydrogen bomb is the deadliest weapon ever developed because it can kill hundreds of thousands of people and obliterate whole cities. **Better:** The hydrogen bomb, which can kill hundreds of thousands of people and obliterate whole cities, is the deadliest weapon ever developed.

Combining short sentences that discuss identical or very closely related issues builds stronger links between ideas and eliminates some of the stop-and-go choppiness that exists with two separate sentences. The subject in the second sentence does not have to be the same word-for-word subject found in the first sentence; it can just as easily be a pronoun reference or a characterization that uses different words to describe the same thing.

> The Clayton Act was passed in 1914 after a bitter fight in Congress. This act was a supplement to the Sherman Act and specified ... *In this paper, the most important information and the focus of the paragraph was on what the legislation accomplished.* **Better**: The Clayton Act, which was passed in 1914 after a bitter fight in Congress, was a supplement to the Sherman Act and specified ...

> The Beatles transformed pop music and studio recording. They were constantly seeking the next great sound and composed in a variety of styles. **Better:** The Beatles, who were constantly seeking the next great sound and composed in a variety of styles, transformed pop music and studio recording.

> Milton's portrayal of Satan creates an image in the reader's mind of an epic character. This larger-than-life personality leads his fallen angels in a decisive battle. **Better:** Milton's portrayal of Satan creates an image in the reader's mind of an epic character, a larger-than-life personality who leads his fallen angels in a decisive battle.

> King called for a nonviolent campaign for peace. He organized parades, sit-ins, and marches. **Better**: King called for a nonviolent campaign for peace that organized parades, sit-ins, and marches. *The nonviolent campaign is more meaningful to the reader when the sentences are combined.*

If a first sentence notes an action, development, or situation and the next sentence provides specifics, the details in the second sentence should be worked into the first sentence to create a more meaningful sentence provided this can be done without jeopardizing clarity. Sentences that begin with the "the reason for" can easily be folded into the previous sentence by inserting a "because" clause.

Just a few days ago, Al-Shabaab attacked the Presidential Palace in Mogadishu. The method used by Al-Shabaab in this attack was a car bomb followed by small arms fire. **Better**: Just a few days ago, Al-Shabaab attacked the Presidential Palace in Mogadishu with a car bomb followed by small arms fire.

Another form of discrimination also affected Buddhists and Christians who served in South Vietnam's military. They could not advance beyond a certain rank unless they converted to Roman Catholicism. **Better**: Another form of discrimination did not allow Buddhists and Christians who served in South Vietnam's military from advancing beyond a certain rank unless they converted to Roman Catholicism.

The student population in my elementary teaching assignment was highly diverse. We had 14 special education students in grades two through four, most of whom were working at different levels. **Better**: The student population in my elementary teaching assignment was highly diverse and consisted of 14 special education students in grades two through four, most of whom were working at different levels.

PCs are still very vulnerable. The reason this is so is because when a new PC is purchased it comes with "easy to use" software, and "easy to use means easy to break in" for hackers. **Better**: PCs are still very vulnerable because when a new PC is purchased it comes with "easy to use" software, and "easy to use" means easy to break in for hackers.

When *this* refers to the main idea of a preceding sentence/independent clause, try deleting *this* and write one sentence with the main entity or concept in the first sentence/first independent clause serving as the basis for the subject in the rewritten sentence. The connection between the two main ideas will be strengthened, and a more direct, graspable sentence will emerge.

> Mike Martin had an extensive background in recording sound effects in comedy records, and this helped The Beatles to "push their compositional limits." **Better**: Mike Martin's extensive background in recording sound effects in comedy records helped The Beatles to "push their compositional limits."

Sentences with *this* and *these* as subjects that include only descriptive or explanatory material tend to give the writing a plodding, halting feel. They also require the reader to pause and process exactly what the writer means by *this* and *these*. The use of a noun or a participle phrase can eliminate this second sentence. Similarly, when *this* and *these* lead a second sentence that provides examples, try using a "such as" or an *including* phrase and eliminate the separate sentence. If the list of examples is long, stick with a second, separate sentence.

> The quick ratio for Big Machines Inc. was only 0.75 in 2014. This is an excellent metric for a company that produces multi-million-dollar machinery. **Better**: The quick ratio for Big Machines Inc. was only 0.75 in 2014, an excellent metric for a company that produces multi-million-dollar machinery.

> If Thai firms are to compete globally, they need to focus on competencies that are associated with improved international performance. These include business diversification, development of new international markets, and greater innovation. **Better**: If Thai firms are to compete globally, they need to focus on competencies that are associated with improved international performance, such as business diversification, development of new international markets, and greater innovation.

> A noun phrase is a phrase that includes a noun (as the key word) and its modifiers, both adjectives and other phrases.
>
> A participle phrase is a phrase that modifies a noun and usually ends in –ing or –ed.

If you use *this* or *these* as a stand-alone subject for two different ideas, identify exactly what *this* is referencing in the previous sentence and make sure it fits as a subject for both ideas in the second sentence. Otherwise, you may miss a potential disconnect because an amorphous *this* will fit with almost anything until it is defined.

> While the Egyptians preferred to quarry large stones, the Greeks preferred using smaller, more manageable-sized stones. This *(the use of smaller, more manageable-sized stones)* allowed for blocks to be moved by an ox team *(so far so good)* and the construction of larger statues from smaller stones *(huh?)*. *Replacing "this" with the specific reference helped to identify the redundancy "from smaller stones."*

The flow of two sentences, the second of which includes the construction "after this, X occurred," can be improved. Move *after* to the front of the first sentence and write one sentence. Such sentences almost always can be combined. The phrase "before then" is another construction that can similarly be improved to strengthen the connection between ideas.

> HCM Beverages was formed after the Vietnamese government changed its economic policies and the United States lifted its restrictions on business in Vietnam. After this, most locally owned bottling companies in Vietnam formed joint-ventures with foreign partners. **Better:** After the Vietnamese government changed its economic policies and the United States lifted its restrictions on business in Vietnam, most locally owned bot-

tling companies in Vietnam formed joint-ventures, such as HCM Beverages, with foreign partners.

Using the adjectives "this" and "these" links ideas and entities between sentences and helps to maintain continuity between sentences. Another simple linking technique is to use the phrase "for example" when citing a specific illustration of a general point that has been made. "Similarly" is a good word choice to start a new sentence that is either citing another example or making a new but similar point.

The two atomic bombs dropped on Japan had as much destructive power as the combined bomb payload of 2,000 B-29s. The implications of ~~the~~ **this** destructive power for the future of mankind were enormous.

The Roman Empire endured for hundreds of years and spanned hundreds of miles across several continents. Roman influence, for example, extended from northern Europe as far as England south to Africa and the Middle East.

ELIMINATE (OR MINIMIZE) READERS' UNCERTAINTY

Uncertainty in how to interpret ideas and information in a sentence slows the reader down. If the meaning is not clear, the reader often will reread the sentence. Minimize the space between what you were thinking when you wrote the sentence and what the reader might conceivably take away from the sentence. When this space grows too large, the reader can get stuck trying to decode what you meant to say. Every sentence in your paper is a potential quagmire for your reader. There are several ways to put distance between your thoughts and the reader's interpretation of your thoughts that you want to avoid: references that can have multiple interpretations, slang and colloquial expressions, words that only half fit; failing to explain a view or complete a thought; and leaving out key information. The problem can involve just one word, a term consisting of several words, or a phrase or clause that makes up a good portion of the sentence.

Elaborate When in Doubt. Strive to make your writing as concise as possible without sacrificing clarity. In some situations, however, a short reference of a few words is not an option because the reference is ambiguous (or inaccurate as in the first example below) and needs more explanation, often in a phrase. The reader may be able to sort out the ambiguity, but it will take time. Sometimes, the reader cannot sort it out because there are too many possible interpretations. Readers may be able to guess correctly if a sentence contains one cryptic reference. If a sentence has more than one unclear reference, as in the third example below, the math is not in the reader's favor. The number of possible interpretations of the sentence's main point increases to at least four and possibly six; the sentence is unreadable.

Two teams tied for first in a division made the playoffs if their records were better than all <u>non-division-winners</u> in the league. *What did the non-division-winner win? There is almost no getting around stopping and trying to figure out what is meant by "non-division-winners."* **Better**: Two teams tied for first in a division made the playoffs if their records were better than the records of all the other teams in the league that were not division winners.

The author asserts that his study remains the "most prominent empirical study" of drug use in America, despite its shortcomings <u>in measuring</u> a phenomenon that is often hidden. *What kind of shortcoming in measuring?* **Better:** The author asserts that his study remains the "most prominent empirical study" of drug use in America despite its tendency to underestimate

a phenomenon that is often hidden.

To compete with <u>offshore companies,</u> garment companies in Los Angeles hired <u>foreign workers</u> already living in the United States. Possible interpretations of this sentence: To compete with US companies operating factories abroad, garment companies in LA hired illegal immigrants. **Or:** To compete with foreign companies in other countries, garment companies in LA hired illegal immigrants. **Or:** To compete with US companies operating factories abroad, garment companies in LA hired foreign citizens living in the US legally. **Or:** To compete with foreign companies in other countries, garment companies in LA hired foreign citizens living in the US legally. **Or:** To compete with foreign companies in other countries and US companies operating factories abroad, garment companies in LA hired illegal immigrants. **Or:** To compete with foreign companies in other countries and US companies operating factories abroad, garment companies in LA hired illegal immigrants as well as foreign citizens living in the US legally.

Slang and colloquial expressions, which are unique to a particular culture or generation, are easy to misinterpret. When writing for a broad audience that includes a mix of cultural and generational backgrounds, paraphrase. If you decide to use a colloquial expression, add a phrase that defines the expression. In some cases, the proper English word is the only alternative if inserting a definition is likely to appear excessive and even ludicrous to many readers.

> Winnie gave Verloc <u>a shout out</u> over his promotion to Assistant Commissioner. **Better**: Winnie gave Verloc a shout out—a public expression of recognition—over his promotion to Assistant Commissioner.

> <u>Right</u> after being sworn into office, Truman ... **Better:** <u>Immediately</u> after being sworn into office, Truman ...

Convey the Full Meaning. A key word sometimes only half fits with the rest of the sentence and appears stilted given what is being discussed. The word may not convey the full force of what is happening or what is motivating people to act a certain way. Words that only half fit require the reader to figure out the other half. A longer phrase is sometimes necessary to adequately express the idea when a suitable substitute for the half-fitting word does not exist. To identify nouns that only half fit, insert an appropriate adjective in front of the noun. If the language sounds even odder, a better fitting noun or noun phrase most likely is needed.

> The women in the novel are selflessly motivated by a strong desire to care for their [loving] <u>dependents</u>. **Better**: The women in the novel are selflessly motivated by a strong desire to care for those they love, their husband and their children.

> Goya's dark paintings were inspired by the political <u>surroundings</u> in Spain during his lifetime. Goya's dark paintings were inspired by the [chaotic] political <u>surroundings</u> in Spain during his lifetime. **Better**: Goya's dark paintings were inspired by the chaotic political situation in Spain during his lifetime.

The Founding Fathers probably could not have imagined that the US Constitution would serve as a model for <u>civilizations</u> two hundred years later in Eastern Europe. **Better**: The Founding Fathers probably could not have imagined that the US Constitution would serve as a model for Eastern European countries two hundred years later.

Adjectives can also leave a reader uncertain of the exact meaning, especially adjectives that make qualitative comparisons, such as the worst or the best, with little or no specificity. Provide a short but more detailed description of the comparison.

The September 2013 terrorist attack at the Westgate Mall in Nairobi, Kenya, the <u>worst</u> since the 1998 bombing of the American Embassy in that country, … *Does "worse" refer to economic impact, the total number of wounded and killed, or the total killed?* **Better:** The September 2013 terrorist attack at the Westgate Mall in Nairobi, Kenya, the *most deadly* attack since the 1998 bombing of the American Embassy in that country, …

Many countries are putting in place mechanisms that would stifle <u>free</u> information flows on the internet. *Is the writer saying that users would be charged a fee to use the internet?* **Better**: Many countries are putting in place mechanisms that would stifle the sharing of information on the internet outside of government control.

Provide an Explanation for Your View. Provide a basis for your view even if the view is in a clause and is not the sentence's main idea. The more specific and arcane the issue, the more likely some readers will lack the knowledge to understand the view. A judgment, for example, that compares the Beatles with Frank Sinatra is more likely to be understood than a judgment comparing two songs by the Beatles. A short phrase is all that may be needed. Also remember papers are read from front to back. If you have not yet given the reader the information needed to understand a point you are making, the point is not going to be meaningful at that place in the paper unless you provide that information.

> <u>While some might have difficulty with "Yellow Submarine" and "Tomorrow Never Knows" appearing on the same album</u>, both songs use musique concrete, linking them together. **Better**: While some might have difficulty with "Yellow Submarine" and "Tomorrow Never Knows" appearing on the same album given their vastly different themes, both songs use musique concrete, linking them together.

> Although Laura's curiosity towards the Goblins' fruit is not un-like Eve's curiosity in the Garden of Eden, <u>comparing Lizzie to Jesus Christ is ascribing far too great a meaning to the text.</u> *The reason for anyone to even consider such a comparison was not explained until the middle of the next paragraph.* **Better**: Although Laura's curiosity towards the Goblins' fruit is not unlike Eve's curiosity in the Garden of Eden, comparing Lizzie, who is trying to dissuade her sister from sex and sinning, to Jesus Christ is ascribing far too great a meaning to the text.

Also, when you conclude that something is not as it seems or is akin or like something else, provide a short explanation that tells the reader what it is and how that relates to what it is not. Without an explanation, the judgment will seem like an unsupported assertion and convey nothing of value.

Include Ownership for Views and Actions. When you introduce a new view, belief, perception, or the like, identify the person or group that holds or shares that view. Without that information, the view being discussed raises more questions than it answers. A view or perception is not at all meaningful to the reader without information on who or what group holds the view. Similarly, identify the individual or group that takes an action that is noted for the first time.

When the price of a product is continually discounted, <u>its desirability</u> can decline. **Better:** When the price of a product is continually discounted, its desirability among high-end consumers can decline. *Low-income groups probably have a much different perspective.*

<u>The perception</u> that the US is the great Satan ... *A number of countries and groups view the US as the great Satan.* **Better:** The perception among extremists in Iran that the US is the great Satan ...

The photograph of the Buddhist monk's self-immolation was taken by Malcolm Browne. The picture <u>was immediately sent</u> to the United States for publication in papers there. *If it was important to note who took the photograph, who sent the picture to the US where it set off a firestorm of public commentary is also important.*

If different groups hold conflicting views or the source of the information could conceivably vary, identification of the owner of the view is very important.

The leading suspect in the murder, identified as John Doe, ... *The identification of the suspect could have been provided by a newspaper, district attorney, or even a neighbor of John Doe.* **Better**: The leading suspect in the murder, identified by police as John Doe, ... **Or:** The leading suspect in the murder, whom police identified as John Doe, ...

Elaborate on Details that May Lack Meaning for the Reader. If the facts and details are not widely known, provide a larger context for the details so readers are able to understand their significance. Unless you are certain your readers are familiar with the details, err on the side of caution and provide additional information. What is the point of writing a well written sentence if the reader cannot fully appreciate all of the information in it? In the first example below, some additional geographical context is needed unless all your readers are from southern California.

Seventy-two Thai workers, who were smuggled into the United States, were discovered after a federal raid on a factory in El Monte. *Where is El Monte?* **Better:** Seventy-two Thai workers, who were smuggled into the United States, were discovered after a federal raid on a factory in El Monte, California.

More strict gun controls might have prevented the 2007 incident at Virginia Tech. The shooter bought most of his ammunition by mail order. **Better**: More strict gun controls might have prevented the 2007 incident at Virginia Tech in which 39 students were shot and killed while attending class.

Clarify New Terms and Murky Characterizations and References. The introduction of a new term to describe a previously introduced concept may cause the reader to momentarily pause to figure out the connection (or lack of connection) between the two terms. Linking the new term back to the previous term with a pronoun modifier such as "this" or "these," as well as other modifiers, helps to limit the uncertainty if there is a connection. Another, perhaps better, approach is to not switch terms.

This paper will use panel data analysis to explore the causes of corruption, especially the structural and institutional factors that contribute to this problem. It will then develop policy recommendations by utilizing the data to identify the variables that have the most impact. *Impact on what exactly?* **Better:** This paper will use panel data analysis to explore the causes of corruption, especially the structural and institutional factors that contribute to this problem. It will then develop policy recommendations by utilizing the data to identify which of *these structural and institutional* variables have the most impact on fostering corruption.

The reader also will have to pause to decode poorly defined, broad characterizations. If more than one possible explanation exists, the reader may pick the wrong one. Do not settle for a characterization that, in addition to being confusing, is awkward and stilted. Make the effort to be meticulous.

Buddhists in Vietnam under the Diem government were not allowed to fly Buddhist flags. The Catholic flag, however, was not subjected to the same censorship. Thus, a group of people who <u>fell under the same category</u> but held different religious beliefs could not show their pride and love for their religion. *What category was that?* **Better:** Thus, a group of people who were citizens of Vietnam but held different religious beliefs could not show their pride and love for their religion.

If the sentence contains a pronoun, will the reader immediately know who or what is being referenced? Pronouns that reference people are not the only pronouns that can be misread. "It" can be misunderstood as easily as "they." In addition, when citing a quote that includes a pronoun, will the reader know what or whom the pronoun is referencing? If the pronoun can be misread, make it clear by inserting the specific noun using parentheses after the pronoun in the quote, or by beginning the quote after inserting the specific noun. If the information is important enough to quote, getting the attribution correct in the quote is just as important. Someone reading your report may use this information in their report.

A US study led by Adam Palmer, the head of cybersecurity for Wal-Mart, concluded that 50,000 PCs are infected by malware every hour and that the United States loses around \$32 billion annually due to cyber-crime. What makes this threat so scary is malware/viruses are not limited to PCs; any mobile device is a potential target. Palmer also claims that "from 2009 to 2010, <u>we</u> tracked an almost 100-percent increase in web-based attacks." *If the data refers to the US study, the "US study" should be the subject in the last sentence. If it does not, "Wal Mart" should be.*

References to geographical place names should be consistent with their historical designation at the time: During 1837-45, large numbers of Americans flocked to ~~Texas~~ what was then the Republic of Texas. References that identify the location of geographic entities in their current context should acknowledge that fact: Luna, located in what is now northern Italy, ...

Complete Incomplete Thoughts. A whole range of ideas are not complete unless the context is provided, the choices are specified, or details are added. These missing components raise questions in the reader's mind. Sometimes, the sentence and paragraph contain enough information for the reader to make an educated guess, but not always. Complete the thought.

Emotions, motives, decisions, and preferences are just a few examples of general concepts that almost always require a complement to be complete. Open-ended thoughts can come in a variety of forms, including verbs that do not make much sense if an object of the verb is missing.

Chris McCandless did not want to be controlled by some psychological <u>pressure</u> that plans out his entire day. *The result of the pressure is the planning out of the entire day, but what pressure is driving that?* **Better**: Chris McCandless did not want to be controlled by some psychological pressure to conform that plans out his entire day.

With <u>motivated</u> effort, Diem led the movement to create the Republic of Vietnam, which was vehemently anti-communist. **Better**: Motivated by his deep hatred of communism and his desire to defend Catholicism, Diem led the movement to create the Republic of Vietnam, which was vehemently anti-communist.

When reviewing your paper, look for open-ended thoughts that need closing. Finding and fixing these thoughts <u>will help</u>. *How?* **Better**: Finding and fixing these thoughts will help you write more readable sentences.

ELIMINATE (OR MINIMIZE) DISCREPANCIES

If you want the reader to accept your views and interpretations, the ideas and the basis for them need to be coherent and generally plausible. Sentences that posit outrageous or greatly exaggerated ideas may appear to the reader as incoherent rambling. They diminish the author's credibility. Readers may wonder whether the author believes the idea or whether the idea as stated is just an error or an oversight, perhaps the result of mental sloppiness. Neither perception helps the writer's cause. Sentences that equate unlike items or make misleading comparisons befuddle the reader. The discrepancy in some poorly defined comparisons can be so large that the issue being compared is not at all clear to the reader. Discrepancies also occur when examples are cited to support an

idea but appear unrelated to the idea. References to timing and numbers need to be consistent across sentences.

Correct Careless and Senseless Lapses. Does anything stand out as totally out of kilter when you read the sentence? Is it funny but was not meant to be? Is it even possible? You may need to add one word or several words to convert the nonsense to what you meant to convey. Omit a key part of any idea, and nonsense usually is the outcome. Pay close attention to noun phrases. They may include most of the words related to the concept you are trying to convey, but if the order of words is awry, the phrase will describe something entirely different, as in the second example below. Inappropriately using an adjective to describe possession that does not exist, as in the third example, conveys a completely inaccurate idea

> The Supreme Court's decision to allow resale price maintenance practices will enable manufacturers <u>to terminate retailers</u> that sell competitors' products. *Who would want to do business with those manufacturers?* **Better:** The Supreme Court's decision to allow resale price maintenance practices will enable manufacturers to terminate their business relationships with retailers that sell competitors' products.

> The legislation, nonetheless, represented a major step forward <u>in garment regulation</u>. *Was the government moving to regulate personal decisions on dress?* **Better**: The legislation, nonetheless, still represented a major step forward in regulation of the garment industry.

> Under the non-communist government of President Diem, Buddhists were put in <u>communist prisons</u> without a trial. *Wording suggests the prisons belonged to the communists.* **Better**: Under the non-communist government of President Diem, Buddhists were

sentenced without a trial and sent to prisons built to hold primarily communists.

Modify or Delete Grossly Exaggerated Content. Ask yourself whether the idea as written is credible or just a wild exaggeration. Is the idea so general that the reader has nothing against which to evaluate its plausibility? Take the time and make the effort to be more exact. Grossly inaccurate content can reduce the reader's perception of your thoroughness and reliability, potentially undermining his or her receptivity to other points in the paper that are more valid. The reader is left with the impression that you have not given much thought to the issue, a bad place for a writer to be. In some cases, the exaggerated content cannot be modified to make it accurate and needs to be deleted.

Opposed to violence and aware of the failure of non-violent demonstrations to bring about change in Vietnam, Buddhists monks began to set themselves on fire, an action that they <u>knew would forever alter the world and the hearts of people</u>. *If the writer believed this is what the monks believed, some sense of how the monks thought this would play out is needed.* **Better**: Opposed to violence and aware of the failure of non-violent demonstrations to bring about change in Vietnam, Buddhists monks began to set themselves on fire, an action that they hoped would shock the world, create sympathy for their cause, and pressure the Vietnamese government to implement reforms.

The current modus operandi of terrorism, which is now based largely on explosions, will not last forever. <u>When explosions don't frighten people anymore</u>, new ways to scare people, such as cyber-terrorism, will be used. *When will explosions no longer frighten people?* **Better**: The current modus operandi of terrorism, which is now based largely on explosions, will evolve as new ways to scare people, such as cyber-terrorism, are added to the terrorist's arsenal.

Equate Like Items and Contrast Analogous Issues. In sentences in which the subject (call it A) is being likened to something else (call it B), the subject and the something else must be analogous. If they are not, the main point in the sentence is totally lost because the reader does not know whether the sentence is about A or B. Take the time to accurately and completely write the comparison you want to make.

> In recent decades, the retail industry has been one of the strongest indicators of American economic strength. **Better:** In recent decades, growth in the retail industry has been one of the strongest indicators of American economic strength. **Or:** In recent decades, the retail industry has been one of the strongest sectors in the American economy.

Sentences that compare should compare like items. Few writers will compare items that are totally unrelated, but many inexperienced writers will make inappropriate comparisons of related items. If you are comparing an aspect of X with an aspect of Y, write that comparison in its entirety. A comparison of X with an aspect of Y is not a legitimate comparison. Writing the appropriate comparison often requires more words to include the fuller description of what is being compared. Complete the comparison.

> Business decisions on whether to devote resources to risk management should compare <u>unfavorable outcomes</u> to the <u>cost of the risk management programs</u> themselves. *How is that comparison going to contribute to a better decision?* **Better:** Business decisions on whether to devote resources to risk management should compare the savings gained by minimizing the impact of unfavorable outcomes to the cost of the risk management programs.

The two atomic bombs dropped on Japan had as much <u>destructive power</u> as <u>2,000 B-29s</u>. *Were the B-29s being used as Kamikaze-like weapons?* **Better**: The two atomic bombs dropped on Japan had as much destructive power as the combined bomb payload of 2,000 B-29s.

The <u>Jubilee Church</u> treats the programmatic requirements of the building type very differently than <u>other builders and architects</u> of the past. *How good an architect was the Jubilee Church?* **Better:** The architect of the Jubilee Church treats the programmatic requirements of the building type very differently than other builders and architects of the past.

Pronouns can be vague, especially when used in comparisons. A pronoun used as the subject in the second clause of a comparison refers back to the main entity/idea being compared in the first clause. If it refers to something else, the pronoun needs to be replaced with a specific noun.

Whereas some may find the contrast between the old, low income housing projects and the beautiful new white church disturbing, <u>it</u> adds to the aesthetic value of the surrounding area with its magnificent architecture. *"It" in this sentence refers to the "contrast."* **Better:** Whereas some may find the contrast between the old, low income housing projects and the beautiful new white church disturbing, the church adds to the aesthetic value of the surrounding area with its magnificent architecture.

Clauses that begin with "although," "even though," "whereas," "rather," or "despite" should highlight an opposite idea or an apparent incongruity. These words signal to the reader that an opposite idea will follow in the main part of the sentence. If an opposite idea is not forthcoming, the sentence will appear like a non-sequitur to the reader. Making a distinction between two issues that are not related confuses the reader, who may wonder what he or she overlooked or did not process when reading the sentence: The man was arrested for driving while intoxicated, but he was a resident of Maine. Versus: The man was arrested in Virginia for driving while intoxicated, but he was a resident of Maine.

In some cases, the comparison is implicit, as in the third example below, but making the comparison explicit helps the reader to understand more completely the difference you are highlighting.

Despite investing heavily in establishing a franchise in Somalia, Al Qaeda also experienced significant difficulties. *Significant difficulties in what?* **Better**: Despite investing heavily in establishing a franchise in Somalia, Al Qaeda had little success in recruiting new members. **Or**: Despite overcoming many obstacles in establishing a franchise in Somalia, Al Qaeda also experienced significant difficulties that it could not overcome.

Although the newspaper reporters support their view on the prime minister's mental health with some evidence and outside sources, they are simply espousing their personal opinion. *Nothing is being compared here. That the reporters are espousing their personal opinion is implicit in the first clause.* **Better**: Although the newspaper reporters support their view on the prime minister's mental health with some evidence and outside sources, they do not provide enough evidence to make a convincing case.

The self-immolation of Thich Quang Duc is not just a story about a monk dying, but a monk who was an important figure to other Buddhists as well as to other Vietnamese. *Without a more explicit comparison, the first independent clause in the sentence could just as well be deleted, and the loss in meaning would be negligible: The self-immolation of Thich Quang Duc is a story about a monk dying who was an important figure to other Buddhists as well as to other Vietnamese.* **Better**: The self-immolation of Thich Quang Duc is not just a story about an obscure, little known monk dying, but a monk who was an important figure to other Buddhists as well as to other Vietnamese.

Similarly, a clause that begins with "in addition" should highlight an idea that is analogous to the idea that follows in the main sentence. Otherwise, the clause makes little sense. Most of the time, the clause just needs further elaboration to be comparable with the idea in the main sentence.

In addition to the growing number of mobile devices, PCs also remain very vulnerable to a range of hacking devices and techniques. **Better**: In addition to the growing number of mobile devices that are vulnerable to hacking, PCs also remain very vulnerable to a range of hacking devices and techniques.

A *because* clause that attempts to explain the rationale for one side's opposing view is confusing when the clause lacks a subject or pronoun. This construction is typically found in sentences that compare two sides' negotiating positions. Readers cannot tell which side is citing the rationale in the sentence as the basis for its view. Some readers may be able to correctly interpret the sentence by rereading the sentence and relying on their knowledge of the issue. If the reader lacks this knowledge, he or she may not know what to take away from the sentence, irrespective of how many times the reader rereads the sentence.

A participle phrase led by *citing, claiming,* or an equivalent participle unambiguously links the rationale for a view to the party that holds that view. Locate this phrase immediately before or after the party to which it applies.

> The Brazilian firm proposed much lower salaries than the German firm was willing to accept for its employees working in Brazil because of the lower cost of living in Brazil. **Better:** The Brazilian firm, taking into account the lower cost of living in Brazil, proposed much lower salaries than the German firm was willing to accept for its employees working in Brazil.

> Japan wanted a larger navy than the US was willing to concede because of Japan's dependence on imports of raw materials. **Better**: Japan, citing its dependence on imports of raw materials, wanted a larger navy than the US was willing to concede.

When there is a pronoun or pronoun modifier in a "because" clause that explains one entity's view relative to another entity's view, make sure the pronoun refers to the correct noun. If it does not, the comparison will not make any sense because the explanation for the view will apply to the wrong entity. The explanation for the difference of views that follows in a "because" clause should address the view of the subject of the preceding clause.

> England was less concerned about the threat from Germany than France was because of its disadvantage in Dreadnought battleships. *"Its" refers to England which had an advantage in Dreadnought battleships.* **Better:** England was less concerned about the threat from Germany than France was because of its advantage in Dreadnought battleships.

Discrepancies can also occur between sentences, clauses, and phrases that posit a choice. If the choices are not comparable, the sentence is open to different interpretations. The choice needs to be comparable if a choice has yet to be made. Otherwise, the sentence will read as if a decision has been made and there is no choice, as in the example below. The reader may be able to read between the lines to establish whether a decision has been made, but why ask the reader to do this? The more you adopt a rigorous approach to writing exactly what you mean, the less likely you will accept language than is not as easy for the reader to decipher.

> Rather than abandoning negotiations with Sakari for a new partner, Nora ... **Better:** Rather than abandoning negotiations with Sakari and look for a new partner, Nora ...

Include Language in Examples that Links to the General Point. Examples should use language that clearly shows a connection to the sentence's general point the examples are intended to support. If the ideas appear unrelated, the examples will just befuddle the reader and detract from the credibility of the general point. Sometimes, the solution calls for inserting additional language when the idea is partially there, and sometimes, the language in the examples is so off base that starting over is the only option.

> Stalin was highly insecure as evidenced by his killing of many people in his inner circle during the Great Purge. *Maybe Stalin killed these people because he was just a bloodthirsty tyrant.* **Better:** Stalin was highly insecure as evidenced by his killing of many people in his inner circle, whom he probably viewed as potential rivals or capable of turning on him.

> Even when the characters in the novel seem as though they are acting on behalf of others' needs, such as Mr. Jones taking direction from his wife, ... **Better:** Even when the characters in the novel seem as though they are acting on behalf of others' needs, such as Mr. Jones pursuing better medical care for his wife, ...

Fix or Explain Real and Apparent Disconnects. The ideas in a sentence or paragraph need to make sense when taken together. Disconnects can occur in two forms, real and apparent. Both require some changes to be made to the text. Real disconnects may require only a slight modification of the text to produce a more accurate sentence. Ironically, apparent disconnects usually require a more substantial revision. They will raise questions in the reader's mind that need to be answered. Life does not always make sense and explaining these discrepancies often requires at least a clause or phrase and sometimes, another sentence.

Real disconnects:

The question of whether Napoleon was seeking to develop external or internal power went unanswered in England, but became an assumption that external power meant revolutionary power. *How a question that went unanswered became an assumption defies logic if one assumes that an assumption is a point of view or judgment.* **Better**: The question of whether Napoleon was seeking to develop external or internal power went unanswered in England. In debating this question, English officials assumed that external power meant revolutionary power.

Most cities in Greece usually quarried the closest white marbles because their economies could not afford quarrying in more remote locations. *"Usually" implies that sometimes they could.* **Better**: Most cities in Greece usually quarried the closest white marbles because their economies could not afford *extensive* quarrying in more remote locations.

Apparent disconnects:

The book anonymously written by John Doe, who remains a high ranking official in a Protestant Church, is very critical of religious organizations, comparing them to ... *Adding the following sentence helps to clear up the disconnect.* Doe claims that he can do more good to change the Church's ways from inside the church than from outside the Church.

The witness decided to testify for the state in the trial of a major Colombian drug kingpin. He felt certain that the drug king pin, who had a long history of retaliation against informers, would try to kill him. *Adding the phrase "Despite misgivings about his safety," at the start of the sentence prepares the reader for the second sentence.*

Resolve Inconsistencies in Timing and Numbers. Timing discrepancies can occur within sentences and between sentences. If one sentence, for example, suggests something will occur and the next sentence suggests that events have not yet progressed that far, the reader is immediately confused.

A prosecutor in Los Angeles <u>is deciding</u> if the actor John Doe will face a felony charge for his assault of a photographer. Detectives <u>are close</u> to presenting their evidence to the district attorney for a decision. **Better:** A prosecutor in Los Angeles will decide if the actor John Doe will face a felony charge for his assault of a photographer. Detectives are close to presenting their evidence to the district attorney for a decision.

I recommended that teachers next year provide independent work for the special education students until they were able to begin their instruction. **Better:** I recommended that teachers next year provide independent work for the special education students until they are able to begin their instruction.

If one sentence notes a singular item and another sentence refers back to this item as if there is more than one, readers are is not sure whether they missed something. They may go back and reread previous sentences.

Pronouns that modify a noun must also agree with the number noted in the previous reference to this noun. In the second example below, the wrong pronoun misrepresented the facts.

> EverClear Writing Consultants has developed a short, two-day course on improving the writing of individual sentences. The company is now trying to market <u>these courses</u> to government and business entities. **Better:** The company is now trying to market this course to government and business entities.

> Nora submitted a bid for installing digital switching exchanges for 800,000 telephone lines, although it lacked the manpower to fulfill the bid completely on its own. Nora and Sakari, which had discussed for two years the forming of a joint venture, submitted <u>their</u> bid assuming a joint venture would materialize. **Better:** Nora, which had discussed for two years the forming of a joint venture with Sakari, submitted its bid assuming a joint venture would materialize.

USE WORD COMBINATIONS THAT ARE CLEAR AND MAKE SENSE

Individual words in a sentence need to support one another like an arrangement of properly connected I-beams supports a building. A poorly connected I-beam can weaken the whole structure. When words are used together that do not complement each other, confusion follows. The intended meaning is not conveyed or is conveyed poorly because the words describe a muddled concept or relationship. The location of key words in a series of words can make it harder or easier for the reader to grasp the idea being discussed. Sometimes, an aspect of the idea that is being conveyed in a series of words is open to different interpretations unless the words are ordered appropriately. Be careful about juxtaposing words that are not normally used together. The new term may end up sounding like unfamiliar jargon to some readers. Prepositions are important. A poorly chosen preposition can skew the intended meaning.

Appropriately Characterize Nouns and Their Modifiers. Nouns must be able to possess the attributes adjectives subscribe to them. In some cases, the concept represented by the noun and its adjective is silly or incomprehensible. To catch these incongruous word pairs, read the noun and the adjective separately from the rest of the sentence.

Find a more suitable adjective that makes the sentence more meaningful. In the first example below, the more suitable adjective helps to clarify the main idea. The reader does not have to process specific examples to reach a general conclusion about a key element in the sentence. Sometimes, an appropriate adjective is not available, and a different construction, such as an infinitive, is needed, as in the second example.

> Consumers rely on retail outlets to provide <u>physical</u> goods ranging from clothing and shoes to computers and speakers. **Better:** Consumers rely on retail outlets to provide household goods ranging from clothing and shoes to computers and speakers.

With so much <u>prosperous opportunity</u>, the American colonialists became selfish and prioritized their own desires ahead of everything else. **Better**: With so much opportunity to prosper, the American colonialists became selfish and prioritized their own desires ahead of everything else.

When the modifier is a participle or prepositional phrase, a close read is necessary to spot any potential disconnects. Look for dangling modifiers, especially participle phrases at the beginning of sentences. When a disconnect exists between a noun and a prepositional phrase modifying the noun, more than one interpretation may be possible. The reader has no idea what the writer is talking about in the second example below.

Fearing that the governor would veto the bill, the private right-of- action <u>clause</u> in the legislation was pulled from the bill. *What did the clause fear?* **Better**: Fearing that the governor would veto the bill, *the bill's sponsors* pulled the private right-of- action clause of the legislation from the bill.

The cutting edge <u>design</u> of the dress company ... **Better:** The cutting edge design capabilities of the dress company ... **Or:** The cutting edge design of the dress company's manufacturing plant ...

Dangling modifiers are words or phrases that modify a word that is not in the sentence.

Unless the phrase is descriptive (wearing a white hat), a participle phrase should help to explain the intent or motive of the subject when the sentence contains an action verb. If the participle phrase elaborates on some other aspect of the sentence, the connection to the main idea is harder to see, and the information seems irrelevant. Instead of a participle phrase, use an independent clause or a phrase led by "including" to capture this information.

> Shaarawi wrote about her activities outside the home, helping to organize public lectures for women. **Better**: Shaarawi wrote about her activities outside the home and helped to organize public lectures. **Or**: Shaarawi wrote about her activities outside the home, including her efforts to organize public lectures for women.

> To determine if the participle phrase reflects intent, put the information in a *because* clause after the main clause. Does the sentence make sense. If it does, the phrase most likely is being used correctly: Wanting to help women, Shaawari wrote a book about women. Shaawari wrote a book about women because she wanted to help women.

Choose the Most Suitable Preposition. If a preposition does not fit as a logical link between the noun being modified and the object of the preposition, questions about meaning arise, as in the first example below. Either a different preposition or a different object of the preposition is needed. Sometimes, there is no preposition that will fix the disconnect, and the prepositional phrase needs to be replaced with another type of construction.

> One of the most interesting comments <u>of the article</u> was ... *To whom was the article speaking?* **Better:** One of the most interesting comments *in* the article was made by ... **Or:** One of the most interesting comments of the author of the article was ...

> One most likely would feel powerful emotions from seeing the photograph of a monk <u>under immolation</u>. **Better**: One most likely would feel powerful emotions from seeing the photograph of a monk being immolated.

Prepositions that follow a verb or a past participle need to complement the action of the verb or past participle. Find the most appropriate preposition or change the verb or past participle. The wrong preposition can distort the sentence's main idea.

Scientists at Los Alamos developed the atomic bomb <u>through</u> the help of countless labs, universities, and corporations. **Better:** Scientists at Los Alamos developed the atomic bomb *with* the help of countless labs, universities, and corporations.

President Carter was concerned with the long term economic impact of dwindling oil reserves. *This sentence suggests the issue was something President Carter was addressing.* **Better:** President Carter was concerned about the long term economic impact of dwindling oil reserves. *This sentence suggests the issue worried President Carter.* **Or:** President Carter was alarmed by the long term economic impact of dwindling oil reserves.

In conversation, two prepositions together are easily overlooked. In writing, they stick out noticeably. One of them has to go.

When the Spanish, French, and British came [~~over~~] to the New World, the fate of the indigenous population was doomed.

Do Not Ask Verbal Nouns to Do the Impossible. Verbal nouns are derivatives of verbs (reversal, discovery, walking, etc.) that are used as nouns. If they are modified by a prepositional phrase, the object of the preposition must be capable of being acted upon in the way described by the verbal noun. If the verbal noun and object of the preposition are out of sync, the verbal noun or the object needs to be changed for a better fit between the two. Proof reading the verbal noun as a verb can help catch some of these disconnects.

The Supreme Court's reversal of the <u>case</u> ... **Better:** The Supreme Court's reversal of the decision ...

The discovery of a new pace maker after years of research ... **Better:** The development of a new pace maker after years of research ...

Place the Noun in Front of a Long List of Modifiers. If the sentence contains a long list of modifiers in front of a noun, the reader may feel like he or she is stuck in a do loop without any context to evaluate those modifiers. The reader is reading, but nothing much of value is being transmitted. Putting the noun in front of all those modifiers is the best construction for the reader, especially if the modifiers are proper nouns that the reader may not recognize. If the order of these modifiers has no special significance, arranging them in alphabetical order appears to add a little more coherence to the list. Similarly, provide identifying information in front of a long list of examples whose significance may be lost on the reader.

Roman buildings and statues were now made of Luna, Attica, Euboea, Chios, Phrygia, Teos, Paros, Scyros, Numidia, and Egyptian marbles. **Better:** Roman buildings and statues were now made of marble from Attica, Chios, Egypt, Euboea, Luna, Numidia, Paros, Phrygia, and Scyros.

While touring Germany last summer, I visited Augsburg, Munich, Dachau, and Nuremberg, and several other towns and cities in Bavaria. **Better:** While touring Germany last summer, I visited several towns and cities in Bavaria, including Augsburg, Dachau, Munich, and Nuremberg.

Consider whether the sentence's main point needs all the modifiers and examples. If the focus of the sentence is on a general point and not on the specific modifiers or examples, the sentence probably needs only a few of the modifiers/examples. Adding a generalization to the sentence that captures the essence of the main idea underlying all those modifiers provides the reader with more value-added.

> Roman buildings and statues were now made of marble from the far regions of the Mediterranean, as far west as Numidia in what is now Algeria and as far east as the isle of Scyros in the Aegean Sea.

Limit the Use of Nouns as Adjectives. When nouns are used as adjectives, the resulting word pair can sound like senseless jargon unless it is a well understood phrase, such as risk management. These awkward terms are sometimes difficult to decode. Use a prepositional phrase instead. This guideline also applies to geographic names and other proper nouns used as adjectives, especially if the geographic name or proper noun is not well known. The prepositional phrase will allow you to insert useful information that elaborates on the noun. See the second example below.

> Other colors like Sandbox Orange, Radio Flyer Red, and T-ball Green are intended to remind us of memorable experiences during our youth. These <u>color names </u>represent … **Better:** The names of these colors represent …

> From 36 BC to the early second century AD, <u>Luna marble</u> was supplying all of the white marble for Rome. **Better:** From 36 BC to the early second century AD, marble from Luna, an ancient harbor city in what is now northern Italy, was supplying all of the white marble for Rome.

Ensure All Words in a Series Are Consistent with Surrounding Language. Each word in a series needs to be consistent with the term that introduces the series. For example, all the objects of a prepositional phrase must be capable of being used with the noun the prepositional phrase is modifying, not just the first two. Similarly, make sure that each adjective in a series of adjectives is in sync with the noun being modified. In the second example below, a key element of the main idea is open to different interpretations, and the reader has no idea which is the correct one.

Francisco Goya, a Spanish painter, was a dynamic old master who used his impressionistic style to arouse <u>feelings of</u> fear, distress, political controversy, and moral debate. **Better**: Francisco Goya, a Spanish painter, was a dynamic old master who used his impressionistic style to arouse feelings of fear and distress, political controversy, and moral debate. **Or**: Francisco Goya, a Spanish painter, was a dynamic old master who used his impressionistic style to arouse feelings of fear and distress and to create political controversy and moral debate.

Stone-working in the ancient world slowly evolved over time to meet the <u>taste</u>, size, and function requirements of the building project. **Better**: Stone working in the ancient world slowly evolved over time to meet the style, size, and function requirements of the building project. **Or**: Stone-working in the ancient world slowly evolved over time to meet the personal tastes of the owner and the size and function requirements of the building project.

BE CONCISE AND IMPROVE READABILITY

Unless it is very entertaining reading, few people prefer to read a longer report when a shorter one would work just as well. Writing concisely, however, is not just important for saving space and readers' time. It is equally as important, perhaps more important, for clarity. Unnecessarily wordy sentences can muddle the main idea, complicate the sentence structure, and impede the flow of information in a paragraph. Look for language that can be deleted. Then make a decision about whether you should delete that language. If you are an efficient writer, a few additional words here and there are no big deal. In some cases, you may prefer the slightly longer construction. If the sentence is clearer with the language deleted, there is no choice. The problematic language has to go.

Only Include Ideas That Need Including. Redundant ideas, including those that are implied in other ideas in the sentence, can detract from the sentence's readability. Trying to understand differences that do not exist creates confusion and frustrates the reader. The two examples below show how the deletion of unnecessary information makes for a more direct and readable sentence.

In order to understand how the Roman Empire quarried and used marble, we must first understand the pre-imperial influence of past empires and civilizations on trends in the use of marble. *What exactly is the "pre-imperial influence of past empires"?* **Better**: In order to understand how the Roman Empire quarried and used marble, we must first understand the influence of previous empires and civilizations on trends in the use of marble.

Skilled hackers are able to steal information and issue false orders and commands to computers. This means a skilled hacker can disrupt the flow of information and alter it in an attempt to either crash a system or provide inaccurate information to people. *The ability to "disrupt the flow of information and alter it" is implied in the "issuing of false orders and commands."* **Better**: Skilled hackers are able to steal information and issue false orders and commands to computers in an attempt to either crash a system or provide misleading information to people.

Be careful about adding gratuitous language that at first glance does not seem to change much in the way of meaning. For example, linking important information to what may appear to be a much less important qualification can create the impression that the important information held true only in that specific circumstance.

Shaarawi was betrothed to her cousin when she was very young, a situation that she despised <u>at the time</u> but did not resist. *The language suggests Shaarawi may have changed her mind about this situation. Did she?*

Concepts that are implied in other ideas as a beginning step or stage in a process are hard to detect because the language used to describe the two steps is very different and not much is being repeated. Nonetheless, the inclusion of the idea representing the beginning step is not needed when one cannot get to the second idea, call it step B, without first getting to step A. The inclusion of the beginning step makes for a longer, less readable sentence and delays getting to the sentence's main point. A phrase or an adjective that covers both stages may be available, as in the third example.

Over this span of time, civilizations <u>would learn the construction techniques of the past</u>, further adapting them to meet the needs of their current way of life, thereby advancing the evolution of the use of stone. *Learning the techniques is implied in adapting them.* **Better**: Over this span of time, civilizations would adapt the construction techniques of the past to meet the needs of their current way of life, thereby advancing the evolution of the use of stone.

The treatment of women within a society provides important insights into a society's growth and the social, economic, and political changes taking place in a society. *"Growth" and "changes" are the same idea.* **Better**: The treatment of women within a society provides important insights into the social, economic, and political changes taking place in a society.

… a reference to the opposition she first encountered <u>early in her life</u> to her desire for education and continued to face <u>as long as she lived</u>. **Better**: … a reference to the life-long opposition she encountered to continuing her education.

Minimize the Long Windedness. If you can use fewer words to say the same thing, use fewer words. In the two examples below, the more concise variants are more direct and readable.

> The creation of Canada's Federal Government in 1867 has neither translated into improved governance capacity nor the government's effective control over the country's vast territory. **Better**: The creation of Canada's Federal Government in 1867 has neither improved governance nor the government's control over the country's vast territory.

> This paper starts with a discussion of the problem of state collapse in Yemen and the challenges this creates for US national security. It then gives a brief historical overview of the activities of the main terrorist group based in Yemen. **Better**: This paper starts with a discussion of the challenges state collapse in Yemen creates for US national security, and then reviews the activities of the main terrorist group based in Yemen.

Delete unnecessary adjectives that take the focus off the sentence's main point, especially if they are in dependent clauses. Read the sentence without the adjective(s) and ask yourself how much of the sentence's main point was lost. A series of grandiose sounding adjectives is almost always a distraction. If the adjectives serve a specific purpose related to the main point of the sentence, include them. If they do not, delete them or find one adjective that sums up the gist of the idea. Adjectives in the main clause that address a concept that has already been thoroughly discussed also may not be necessary. All of the above also can be said for adverbs. Gratuitous modifiers needlessly complicate a sentence and take time to process.

While communism presented <u>an ongoing, serious, and pervasive</u> threat to these countries, ... *At least two of those adjectives—ongoing and pervasive—require a lot of processing, at least for me.* **Better**: While communism presented a major threat to these countries, ...

The inability of these ~~purportedly democratic~~ governments to maintain order and liberty ... *Previous paragraphs in the paper discussed the authoritarian tendencies of these newly established democracies. "These" is all the sentence needs.*

~~Coincidentally~~ similar to Plato's description of "philosopher kings," Confucianism holds a belief in the "superiority and duty to lead of the educated man." *The main point in this sentence is defining Confucianism. The paragraph was focused on the difficulty of transplanting Western-style democracies to Asian countries. Given this focus, a good case could be made that the entire first clause is a distraction, not just "coincidentally."*

The redundancy of some adjectives and adverbs can be difficult to detect because they seem like such a good fit with the noun or verb they are modifying. Ironically, the better the fit, the more likely the adjective or adverb may not be needed. As a check, insert the antonym of the modifier into the sentence. If it does not fit with the noun or verb, the modifier probably is superfluous.

Rembrandt's ~~actual~~ painting *Supper at Emmaus* is on display at a museum in Paris.

The group publicly claimed that the attack was in ~~direct~~ retaliation for Israel's incursion into Lebanon. *Can you do anything in indirect retaliation?*

To ~~better~~ compete with companies providing a less expensive product ... *Almost everyone competes to win so "better" is implicit and can be deleted.*

My brother ~~successfully~~ passed his the state bar in Virginia last summer and is now practicing law here. *Can you unsuccessfully pass the bar?*

Verbs such as *opt, decide,* and *choose* are often unnecessary when followed by an action. Delete them and make the action the main verb. The adverb *further* is not needed with verbs such as *expanded* and *increased,* unless the idea is to convey a new expansion or increase. Review verb and adverb pairs to see if the adverbs are needed.

The president <u>chose to nominate</u> a divisive and abrasive prime minister. **Better:** The president nominated a divisive and abrasive prime minister.

The marble trade was <u>further expanded</u> to include quarries along the Mediterranean Coast. **Better:** The marble trade was ~~further~~ expanded to include quarries along the Mediterranean Coast.

Inexperienced writers will sometimes use the verb *put* in conjunction with nouns such as pressure or stress. *Put* is often not needed in this context and is a wasted word. Make the direct object of *put* the verb. Save *put* for putting something somewhere.

The director of the institute was putting pressure on the institute's scientists to discover a cure for cancer. **Better:** The director of the institute was pressuring the institute's scientists to discover a cure for cancer.

"It seems" almost always can be replaced with a simpler, more direct construction. Make *seem/seemed* the main verb in the sentence followed by an infinitive, and the sentence will be more direct and have one less clause.

> Although it seems that these ratios indicate an inability to collect credit quickly from costumers ... **Better:** Although these ratios seem to indicate an inability to collect credit quickly from costumers ...

When there is an infinitive following a noun that explains the role or purpose of the noun, inserting *needed* or *required* after the noun is superfluous. Similarly, "was forced" may not be needed if the sentence includes a "*because*" clause that makes *forced* redundant.

> The government lacked enough helicopters needed to perform disaster relief. **Better**: The government lacked enough helicopters to perform disaster relief.

> The government was forced to use helicopters from the oil company because it did not have enough helicopters to conduct relief operations. **Better:** The government used helicopters from the oil company because it did not have enough helicopters to conduct relief operations.

Below are some other examples of commonly used constructions (related to the words *responsible, involves,* and *poses*) that can be tightened:

> Paul McCartney and Yoko Ono were <u>responsible </u>for bringing musique concrete to The Beatles' recording sessions and ... **Better:** Paul McCartney and Yoko Ono brought musique concrete to The Beatles' recording sessions and ...

Musique concrète is an avant-garde compositional technique associated with the Modernist movement that <u>involves </u>recording real-life sounds and manipulating them … **Better:** Musique concrète is an avant-garde compositional technique associated with the Modernist movement that records real-life sounds and manipulates them …

The mobilization of soldiers' on Germany's border <u>poses </u>a threat … **Better**: The mobilization of soldiers' on Germany's border threatens …

Several commonly used phrases are quite popular but unnecessary. The phrase "the fact that" is used all the time and adds nothing. Replace the verb that follows "that" in this construction with a noun that captures the action of the verb.

The fact that Stalin executed dozens of Soviet generals in the 1930s instilled fear in the Soviet officer corps during World War II and guaranteed the loyalty of top commanders. **Better:** Stalin's execution of dozens of Soviet generals in the 1930s instilled fear in the Soviet officer corps during World War II and guaranteed the loyalty of top commanders.

The fact that managers fail to identify risks early enough … **Better:** The failure of managers to identify risks …

A selection of phrases and words that are in the same category is listed below. As a general rule, find alternative language.

"It is important to understand …" and like expressions. If the issue is not important, you would not be addressing it. Get to the point. Example: ~~It is important to understand how~~ the US came to play a major role … (because)

78

in my opinion. "In my opinion" is understood if you are the author.

in the eyes of. The phrase can almost always be scrapped. Example: In the eyes of college students, laws prohibiting alcohol use are unfair and counterproductive. College students perceive laws prohibiting alcohol use as unfair and counterproductive

the combination of. Example: [The combination of] high inflation and lower productivity is (are) …

in all x, whether y or z. Example: … applied to employees in all job sectors, whether public or private. … applied to employees in both the public and private sector.

whether or not. Whether implies or not. The "or not" can be deleted without any loss of meaning. Example: A stock's price/earnings ratio is a good indicator of whether [or not] a company's stock is overvalued.

not only X but also Y. This construction needlessly complicates the sentence. The gain in emphasis that is obtained by using the phrase seems minimal. Example: Building a nuclear weapon that could kill thousands of people in an instant posed a moral dilemma not only for [insert: both] the American government but for and the American people. The "not-only-but" expression is useful when the two elements are modified by a phrase or clause. Example: Completion of the job required not only knowledge of the electrical connections, but also several diagnostic tools that the repairman did not have.

so too did. "Also" is a perfectly good substitute. Example: [So too did] Locke and Rousseau (also) point(ed) out …

are now. Are implies now. If the emphasis is not on the new-ness of the development, *now* can be deleted. Example: India, Singapore and South Korea are [~~now~~] creating technology and manufacturing capabilities that may soon rival Japan's capabilities.

in a [something-like] fashion. Example: Towns supporting the frontier expansion grew into cities in a rapid fashion. Use an adverb. Towns supporting the frontier expansion grew rapidly into cities.

all. "All" is not needed when it follows a list of several subjects, although a lot of writers are fond of using it in this context. Example: Taiwan, South Korea, and the Philippines [~~all~~] ended martial law in the 1980s.

Delete Unnecessary References and Comparisons. Two references in one sentence (or one independent clause) to the same person, thing, or concept can needlessly complicate the sentence and obscure the main point. Review the sentence to see if it can be rewritten with only one of the references. In the second example below, there is ambiguity about how many types of mini-books were created.

I created sticker charts for <u>two of the students</u> to motivate <u>them</u> to complete their work. **Better:** I created sticker charts to motivate two of the students to complete their work.

I developed a lesson plan for <u>making mini-books</u> that includes a book template that I created using KidPix software to facilitate student <u>creation of their mini-books</u>. **Better:** I developed a lesson plan for students to make mini-books using a book template that I created using KidPix software.

A sentence that includes an introductory phrase that identifies the author of a study followed by the main clause that posits the author's views usually only needs the one reference to the author in the main clause. Otherwise, the reader has to process the pronoun reference. In the sentence below, "*he*" could conceivably be a reference to someone being cited in the report and not the author.

In a report by <u>Martin Libicki</u> on cyber deterrence and cyberwar, <u>he</u> claims estimates of the damage from today's cyber-attacks in the United States "range from hundreds of billions of dollars to just a few billion dollars per year." **Better:** In a report on cyber deterrence and cyberwar, Martin Libicki claims estimates of the damage from today's cyber-attacks in the United States 'range from hundreds of billions of dollars to just a few billion dollars per year."

Comparisons that refer back to ideas and information that have been thoroughly discussed are not necessary most of the time. A common construction used to make these comparisons begins with "just as." The names, dates, and actions that follow "just as" are already well known to the reader. Try substituting a short adjective, such as *similar* or *different*, to replace the longer phrase or clause making the comparison.

The fire in the photograph appears as if it is reaching for the other Buddhist monks as if it is foreshadowing a fate that the other monks will also experience <u>just as Thich Quang Doc had</u>. *The entire paper up to this point has been about Thich Quang Doc.* **Better**: The fire in the photograph appears as if it is reaching for the other Buddhist monks as if it is foreshadowing a *similar* fate for the other monks.

Keep Transitional Language to a Minimum. Introductory phrases that introduce background information may contain text that can be deleted. Look for information that is implied or repeated again in the main clause of the sentence. Some introductory phrases will combine new information with old information that is already understood at that point in the paper. Focus the introductory phrase on the new information.

> In terms of focusing international, regional, and domestic efforts toward eradicating corruption, FSU states and those that wish to help them will most likely reap greater dividends by focusing on fostering free press in these countries than by attempting to affect other factors of corruption. **Better**: FSU states and those that wish to help them will most likely reap greater dividends in reducing corruption by fostering free press in these countries than by attempting to affect other factors of corruption. *The introductory phrase is essentially repeated again in "FSU states and those that wish to help them."*

> According to another respondent interviewed for this study, the director of the Center for African Security, Strategic and International Studies, a research think tank linked to the Ugandan military, ... **Better**: According to the director of the Center for African Security, Strategic and International Studies, a research think tank linked to the Ugandan military, ...

Delete unnecessary language in introductory clauses that contrasts a previously discussed idea with a new idea. The reader is already familiar with the previous idea and rehashing it in detail probably is not necessary, especially if that idea and the basis for it was just discussed in the immediately preceding paragraph or sentence. Look for a short phrase to note the contrast or just start with the new idea. Also, do not start a paragraph with a clause that tells the reader an issue will be addressed later in the paper. If the issue is going to be addressed in the paper, the reader will find out soon enough. The notification at that point in the paper is mostly a distraction.

Although the male characters in the novel all displayed excessive selfishness, the female characters in the novel almost always acted out of altruistic motives and concern for others. **Better:** The female characters in the novel, in contrast to the male characters, almost always acted out of altruistic motives and concern for others.

[Before examining the impact of Western democratic roots,] the paper will address ...

Sometimes, unnecessary transitional information can lock the sentence into a passive-voice construction in which the main idea appears to take a "back seat" (relegated in importance) to the transitional information. Remember the first guideline: focus on the main idea.

Shaarawi and Edib emphasized several common themes in their writings. Chief among these agreements is their shared belief that women should receive an education and enjoy other freedoms often denied to them. **Better:** They believed, most importantly, that women should receive an education and enjoy other freedoms often denied to them.

Phrases such as "chief among these" and the "most important difference" provide little, if any, value-added and are difficult to interpret. They appear to suggest that what follows is important, but they do not explain why. The phrase "most importantly" is a good-enough substitute for a weak idea. One could argue that even "most importantly" adds little and is not necessary. The writer's decision to discuss the issue and the order in which the information is presented in the paper are pretty good indicators of the material's importance.

Eliminate (or Fix) Redundancies in Lists. Look for redundant language in a series of individual words or phrases that are intended to provide examples or elaborate. Ask yourself whether all the items in the list are truly unique and separate. Delete the redundant items. If they are intended to be unique but do not read that way, elaborate and more clearly highlight the difference, as in the third example below.

> An accurate assessment of student progress, development, and achievement ... **Better:** An accurate assessment of student progress and achievement ...

> The sales person will have extensive knowledge of all the different brands of sunglasses, which brand is the best buy for your needs, and the characteristics of each brand. **Better:** The sales person will have extensive knowledge of all the different brands of sunglasses and which brand is the best buy for your needs.

> King explains the actions his group took, why they used those actions, and the reasoning behind the timing. **Better:** King explains what was compelling him and his followers to embrace civil disobedience, what they were hoping to accomplish by taking these actions, and why they were taking these actions now.

In some cases, you may have a list where one item is a sub set of another item. Juxtapose these items and add language that indicates that there is a relationship between the two. Do not leave the auxiliary item as a stand-alone item comparable to others in the list. Giving the auxiliary item equal billing in the sentence suggests the item is as important as others in the list when it is not. The accuracy of the sentence's main point is diminished

> The sales person will have extensive knowledge of all the different brands of sunglasses and their characteristics, which brand is the best buy for your needs, and the glare-reducing characteristics of each brand. **Better:** The sales person will

have extensive knowledge of all the different brands of sunglasses and their characteristics, including their glare reducing characteristics, and which brand is the best buy for your needs.

Use the Shorter Apostrophe Modifier if Possible. If the sentence contains a prepositional phrase explaining ownership, consider using an apostrophe modifier in lieu of the prepositional phrase. Similarly, if you have an action noun (decision, inspection, arrival, etc.) and need to show who performed the action, an apostrophe modifier usually is a better option than using a prepositional phrase. The apostrophe modifier establishes a more direct and clear link to the owner or the doer, especially if the sentence includes an intermediate phrase between the noun and prepositional phrase identifying the owner or doer.

> The decision in Jones vs. Jones by the Supreme Court … **Better:** The Supreme Court's decision in Jones vs. Jones …

If the entity possessing ownership or performing the action, however, is composed of a string of several words, which is often the case with the names of organizations, using the prepositional phrase works better and probably is easier for the reader to track.

> The decision by the Legal Department of the US Department of Agriculture …

Replace Short Clauses and Phrases with Adjective(s) If Possible. Some of these clauses work well in conversation where multiple adjectives are seldom strung together, but their usage in written products can sometimes make your writing look less professional if the entire clause can be replaced with a simple adjective. Look for an appropriate adjective and delete the clause or phrase. The shorter the clause or phrase, the more likely it can be replaced with an adjective.

Despite the existence of risk management processes that work ... **Better:** Despite the existence of proven risk management processes ...

The concrete shells are covered with a patented mixture that is self-cleaning ... **Better:** The concrete shells are covered with a patented, self-cleaning mixture ...

Emotions of a human range ... **Better**: Human emotions range ...

A simple adjective can also replace some longer clauses.

The procedure to treat throat cancer requires a set of pulsed emissions of radiation that have to be discharged at perfectly timed increments. **Better**: The procedure to treat throat cancer requires a set of perfectly timed, pulsed emissions of radiation.

Delete Unnecessary "it-is and there-are" Constructions. For some "it-is and there-are" constructions, the *it* or *there* can be deleted and the *is* or *are* moved to another place in the sentence, as in the first example below. In some cases, the *is* or *are* also can be deleted, as in the second example. Identify the key noun in the sentence (or independent clause) and make it the subject in a shorter, more direct construction. If the only option to replacing *there* is the verb *exists*, there is not much difference between the two. Consider sticking with *there*.

It is the narrator's job to provide some deeper insight to the reader about the novel's setting. **Better:** The narrator's job is to provide some deeper insight to the reader about the novel's setting.

There are many other types of technology that can be used in the classroom. **Better:** Many other types of technology can be used in the classroom.

THE BALL IS IN YOUR COURT (IT IS UP TO YOU)

Writing is a skill, and like any skill, there is a learning curve. Systematically and rigorously review and edit every sentence looking for lapses in clarity. When you note a lapse in clarity, identify the cause. That recognition of a lapse in clarity and identification of the cause is key to writing more readable sentences. Then identify a solution: what words need to be added or deleted, what words need to be replaced, and what words need to be moved to another location in the sentence? The next time you encounter a similar problematic sentence, you will immediately know what to do.

Strive to make your sentences as readable as possible. Review your drafts as if you are the reader. Do not allow connections, explanations, and elaborations that are in your mind, but not on paper, to skew your interpretation of how readable a sentence is. If you refuse to allow bits of confusion to remain in your drafts—despite how much time and effort are required to eliminate them—the readability of your sentences will improve. Conversely, if you allow confusion to "slide," improvement will be slow.

How good a writer you become will require attention and hard work. The return on the investment, however, will be well worth the effort. Learning how to write is a gift that keeps on giving. It is like learning how to ride a bike or drive a car. Once you learn, you do not forget.

Good writing skills will be an asset every time you need to write a paper in college and every time an employer asks for a writing sample. These skills will also serve you well throughout the course of your professional career, whether you are writing a major report about an international development or an e-mail to your boss or client about a business proposal.

A Summary Checklist for Reviewing Sentences

Step 1. Review the subject and the verb for focus, directness, compatibility, and completeness. Does the subject and verb focus on the main idea that you want to highlight? Can the subject and verb be simplified and made more direct? Is the verb in sync with the subject and the rest of the sentence? Is the subject complete?

Step 2. Review the sentence for content and effectiveness. Does the sentence deliver on its main point? Does the sentence bounce from one idea to the next? Are all the elements of the main idea there? Does the sentence include language that could be stated more simply? Are the clauses helpful or a hindrance? Does the sentence stop before saying much of value or end where it began? Does the sentence move forward from the preceding sentence?

Step 3. Review the sentence looking for ambiguous, confusing, and incomplete information. Are there key concepts in the sentence that are open to multiple interpretations or word choices that appear to be a poor fit for what is being discussed? Does the reader have all the information he or she needs to understand the point you are making? Does the sentence identify the owner of a view or the performer of an action? Will the reader need more context to understand any of the sentence's details? Are there any references, characterizations, or pronouns that might baffle the reader? Are there any incomplete thoughts in the sentence?

Step 4. Review the sentence for common sense and consistency. Does the sentence appear to state the ridiculous when that is not the intent? Is the main idea plausible or seem more like science fiction? Are comparisons in the sentence complete and analogous? Are there any inconsistencies in the logic between the ideas in the sentence? Is information on timing and numbers consistent with what was said in previous sentences? Do the examples in a sentence link back to the general point or appear to have little relevance to the general point?

Step 5. Review word combinations for appropriateness and clarity. Do all the adjective-noun combinations make sense when they are taken together? Is the preposition a good fit for the noun, adjective, or past participle being modified? Is a noun that is being extensively modified in the best position for the reader? Can this list of extensive modifiers be shortened? Do any word pairs that are using a noun as an adjective read like jargon? Are all the words in a series consistent with what is being modified?

Step 6. Review the sentence for wordiness that hinders the sentence's readability. Does the sentence include information that was already noted earlier in the sentence in some form? Can you delete words without any loss of meaning? Are there are unnecessary references or redundant items in a list? Can you improve the readability of the sentence by using an apostrophe modifier or by replacing a long clause with an adjective?

Appendix: A Few Words Can Help the Reader a Lot

Below is a two-paragraph excerpt from a student paper followed by the same two paragraphs with changes that help to tie the two paragraphs together.

Martin Luther King Jr. was one of the most pivotal civil rights leaders in the 1950s and 60s. As a Baptist Minister, he called for a nonviolent campaign for peace that organized parades, sit-ins, and marches. After he was arrested for parading without a permit in April 1964, eight pastors from Alabama wrote and published a newspaper article entitled "A Call for Unity" in which they criticized King and his methods. King responded to the criticism in a letter called "Letter from Birmingham Jail" in which he argued that to oppose him was to support the violent campaign against segregation. King's letter was effective because of its emotional appeals relating to every black person, examples from other countries' histories, and biblical references.

King's letter is a long response. Compared to the seven-paragraph letter he received, King wrote fifty paragraphs back. King explains what was compelling him and his followers to embrace civil disobedience, what they were hoping to accomplish by taking these actions, and why they were taking these actions now. King explains why he and his followers, according to King's definition of just and unjust laws, thought that breaking the law was a good idea, and King supports his reasoning with logic and examples from the Bible and history. King addresses the white moderates, and tells them how he is disappointed with their failure to act, and he also tells the white church how he is disappointed its members would be so callous to the needs of their brothers. King ends the letters by saying he wishes that he and the pastors would not bear any enmity towards each other, and that he wants to get to know them all personally.

In the first paragraph, there is uncertainty about whether the pastors were white or black. The reference to "emotional appeals relating to every black person" suggests they could be black. In the last half of the second paragraph, the unexpected reference to King's "address to white moderates" and the reference to plural letters in the next sentence suggest King wrote separate letters to white moderates. The second paragraph is much more connected to the first paragraph after establishing that King's letter was addressed to white pastors and eliminating the discrepancy regarding the number of letters.

Martin Luther King Jr. was one of the most pivotal civil rights leaders in the 1950s and 60s. As a Baptist Minister, he called for a nonviolent campaign for peace that organized parades, sit-ins, and marches. After he was arrested for parading without a permit in April 1964, eight <u>white pastors</u> from Alabama wrote and published a newspaper article entitled "A Call for Unity" in which they criticized King and his methods. King responded to the criticism in a letter called "Letter from Birmingham Jail" in which he argued that to oppose him was to support the violent campaign against segregation. King's letter was effective because of its emotional appeals that <u>described the unfairness that every black person had to endure,</u> examples from other countries' histories, and biblical references.

King's letter is a long response. Compared to the seven-paragraph letter he received, King wrote fifty paragraphs back. King explains what was compelling him and his followers to embrace civil disobedience, what they were hoping to accomplish by taking these actions, and why they were taking these actions now. King explains why he and his followers, according to King's definition of just and unjust laws, thought that breaking the law was a good idea, and King supports his reasoning with logic and examples from the Bible and history. King tells the white moderates how he is disappointed with their failure to act, and he also tells the white church how he is disappointed its members would be so callous to the needs of their brothers. King ends the <u>letter</u> by saying he wishes that he and the pastors would not bear any enmity towards each other, and that he wants to get to know them all personally.

Exercises

1. These governments often resorted to authoritarian measures because of the youth of their democracies. *A key element in the main idea
   needs elaboration.*

2. The future of cybersecurity depends largely on nations working together. There is an urgent need to raise the public's awareness of
   the risk and to share information on cyber threats and criminal networks. *First sentence ends too abruptly.*

3. The Civil War and decades of struggling for equality turned our nation into a land of near-infinite freedom. *Sentence includes exaggerated
   content.*

4. Countries in the Horn of Africa, including Somalia, are geographically close to the Arabian Peninsula and North Africa and provide
   an environment for terrorist links. *The subject is incomplete, and a key
   element in the main idea needs elaboration.*

5. It was important for France to conclude an entente with Russia because it would provide Paris with a major ally in a war with Germany.
   Build sentence around a strong subject.

6. Ngo Dign Diem was an extremely dedicated Roman Catholic, who
   was biased against the Buddhist majority in Vietnam. *An important
   adjective only half fits.*

7. Whereas previously The Beatles had used *musique concrète* to reinforce what the music was already accomplishing lyrically and instrumentally, *musique concrète* makes up "Revolution 9" in its entirety. *The
   difference between the two ideas in the two clauses is not entirely clear.*

8. Although unlimited liability was removed from the bill, the legislation still ... *The subject is not complete.*

9. Retailers prefer to sell respectable brands of merchandise because ... *A key adjective only half fits.*

10. Colored marbles were coming into high demand, along with large monolithic columns, because ... *A stronger subject and more direct verb is needed.*

11. South Korea's military feared the spread of communism and in 1961 seized control of the country, which it did not relinquish until 2003. *Emphasis on a secondary idea needs to be scaled back.*

12. The conversational tone given to the narrator makes the story pleasant to read. *An apostrophe modifier would eliminate an awkward phrase.*

13. Edib wrote for a newspaper that was staffed with prominent writers, who worked hard to incorporate Western culture into Turkey, a prestigious position for her to have had. *Sentence needs to be broken up, and one idea is incomplete.*

14. The implementation of new types of stones in larger building projects demanded a change in how the quarries were administered. *The subject fits poorly with the rest of the sentence.*

15. Buddhists and Christians who enrolled in the military ... *The verb in the dependent clause only half fits.*

16. While Montesquieu proposed that three fundamental forms of democracy might exist—democracy, monarchy, and despotism—he posited that each would be suitable depending on the population. *A comparison is not being made here, although the sentence is written as if a comparison is being made.*

17. McAfee researchers collected 100,000 new malware samples daily in 2012. When those numbers are broken down, that is about 69 new malware samples a minute. *Second sentence includes an idea that does not need including, and the sentences can be combined.*

18. The annexation of Egypt increased the use of marble in Rome. *The verb is not in sync with the rest of the sentence.*

19. If governments and populations had valued the role of the individual more, East Asian democracies might have obtained stability sooner and with greater likeness to democracy as it is practiced in the West. *The sentence includes one idea—possibly two--that is not needed and a phrase that can be reduced to an adjective.*

20. China was driven externally almost exclusively by a fear that it was trapped between two unmatchable powers, the Soviet Union and the United States. *Sentence includes two ideas that need elaboration.*

21. After garment workers failed to pass legislation requiring joint liability, … *Sentence includes a careless and senseless lapse.*

22. While the message about the bonds of sisterhood is a satisfactory story in itself, there is much more to be gleaned from Rossetti's Goblin Market. *A "there are" construction can be eliminated to create a more direct sentence.*

23. Although the views along Aruba's beaches are very picturesque, they are remote and have few hotels. *Analogous things are not being compared.*

24. In the novel, the Assistant Commissioner is the intermediate step of the spectrum of selfishness. *The sentence includes an incomplete subject and a concept that only half fits.*

25. The "seagull sound" in the song "Tomorrow Never Knows" is difficult to identify as Paul McCartney's laughter without background information. *An element of the main idea needs elaboration.*

26. Rather than take a firm position, England and France agreed to German's occupation of the Sudetenland. *The comparison is not complete.*

27. Buddhist monks and nuns staged a series of peaceful prayer meetings at An Quang Pagoda. But peace did not bring change or justice. *Second sentence includes an incomplete subject.*

28. The most telling manifestation of Verloc's selfishness is at the end of the novel when he has to tell Winnie about Stevie's death. Rather than ask for forgiveness, Verloc blames Winnie. *First sentence ends too abruptly; the sentences can be combined.*

29. World War II officially began with the German invasion of Poland but the origins of the war can be traced back to the decision by France and England to allow Germany to remilitarize the Rhineland, although some historians do not agree and attribute the origins of the war to the reparations imposed on Germany in 1918. *The sentence shifts direction too much.*

30. The farmer sought a larger land concession than the company was willing to concede because the region's average annual rainfall exceeded 30 inches. *The entity that is citing the rainfall as the reason for its position is not clear.*

31. Does Chris McCandless ever become just like another mega-mall shopper? Maslow's Hierarchy of Needs may help us determine whether Chris and a mall shopper have similar underlying motives. *An element of the main idea is not complete.*

32. The financial stability and positive outlook for CAT is mainly due to the goals of the company. Their goals are to provide industry leading construction equipment to aid in the construction of facilities, while staying ahead of the competition with ever expanding customer support. *The first sentence ends too abruptly, and an idea in the second sentence can be deleted. The sentences can be combined.*

33. Martial law in Taiwan and South Korea ended in the late 1980s when a sweeping effect of "people power" pushed for liberalization and reform. *An element of the main idea is confusing and needs elaboration.*

34. Consciousness is something researchers would rather not talk about because it is what prevents machines from becoming human. Researchers commonly call consciousness the C-word because they do not want to discuss the issue. *Key information is missing.*

35. When academic concepts are taught to English language learners in their minority language while students are learning the majority language ... *Sentence includes murky characterizations, and redundant language complicates the sentence and makes it harder to process.*

36. Marble requires tools and methods that are different from other stones such as limestone. *Sentence includes an incomplete subject and an incomplete comparison.*

37. Shaarawi insisted that her education be continued even as she was told that it was unnecessary for her station in life, going so far as to say "being a female became a barrier between me and the freedom for which I yearned"—a reference to the life-long opposition she encountered to continuing her education. *The participle phrase seems irrelevant to the action of the verb in the main clause. Write two sentences.*

38. While improved labor conditions and wages are necessary to prevent abuse, over regulation of private companies will reduce their profitability. *Two elements of the main idea in the first clause need elaboration to be complete.*

39. The Diem government did not allow Buddhists monks to show their love to their beliefs, prompting some of them to set themselves on fire. *Sentence includes a poor choice for a preposition.*

40. Al Shabaab's transition from an insurgency focused only on national goals to the most powerful Jihadi organization in the region was slow. *Find a stronger verb and build a more direct sentence.*

41. The sculptor in ancient times had to break down the process of creating a statue into a set of clearly defined steps that organized the creation into an ordered process. *Replace the "that" clause with an adjective and build a sentence that is shorter and easier to process.*

42. The company's most important act was the purchase of a patent that provided increased traction and stability for construction equipment. *A key word only half fits.*

43. While the Business and Competitive Analysis textbook does not specifically approach strategy for global companies, many of the frameworks and models it exposes the reader to would benefit Thai technology firms. *The verb in the first clause is not in sync with the rest of the sentence, and the main clause contains unnecessary language that takes the focus off the main point.*

44. The revealed structure of beams and posts inside the building is a complex work of engineering. *A key word only half fits.*

45. Without retail price maintenance agreements, manufacturers would have no control over what price point their products could be sold or how heavily discounted they might be to sell. *Two ideas in the sentence need to be stated more simply and directly.*

46. A narrator's chief task is to bridge the gap between the reader and the story. This involves providing details about the time, place, setting, and characters. *Combine the sentences to improve the connection between the two ideas.*

47. When examining the more plot-central characters ... *Reads like jargon and is hard to process.*

48. CAT's products also can be attributed to other historically significant creations, such as the Hoover Dam and the English Channel. *The verb is not in sync with the rest of the sentence, and a key word in the sentence only half fits.*

49. A machine does not experience happiness when it completes a task that is given to it. Replace the "that" clause with an adjective.

50. The H-bombs developed in the 1950s—some of which were 2 megaton devices—extended out to 20 miles. *The subject is incomplete.*

51. My drawings are not to be interpreted after a single look but to be investigated. *The intended comparison is somewhat obscured because one word does not completely fit.*

52. Life expectancy in America has increased through the discovery of effective medicines and the development of new medical technologies, and is now around 77 years for men and 82 years for women. *Use active voice to write a sentence with one main clause.*

53. The retail industry must deal with fair competition regulations, such as the antitrust laws. *The sentence provides little of value and ends too soon.*

54. One main aspect that is fueling religious terrorism today is the occupation of foreign lands by Western powers. This is what makes the United States homeland, as well as its interests abroad, a focus for terrorists. *First sentence lacks a strong verb, and the second sentence lacks a strong subject. The two sentences can be combined to create a more direct sentence that better reflects the main idea.*

55. The main hall includes portraits of Chew's niece Margret Oswald and nephew Joseph Turner, highlighting Chew's strong relationship with his family. *The main focus of the paper at that point was to describe Chew's relationship with his family, not the hall.*

56. While other artists represented allegorical and traditional landscape paintings, Goya directly confronted his time through political commentary. *Verb in first clause is out of sync with what follows the verb, and the comparison in the sentence is not complete.*

57. During my two-year stay in Greece, I visited the Crete, Euboea, Cephalonia, Lesbos, Chios, Rhodes, Corfu, and Samos islands. *Make the long list of modifiers more intelligible for the reader.*

58. The vast quantity of marble used throughout the Roman Empire clarifies its extensive influence on both the art and architecture. *The verb is out of sync with rest of sentence.*

59. There are surely similarities found between Rossetti's poem and the Bible, but these similarities should be interpreted more as symbols and allusions than bits and pieces of an overarching Bible allegory. *First independent clause has little of substance in it; build the sentence around one main clause and write a more concise sentence that highlights the main point.*

60. Social and economic inequalities in the region are common and lend themselves to terrorist exploitation. *A key element of the main idea needs elaboration.*

61. Several methods that hackers may use to attack your device depend on what it is they are looking to do. *Find a stronger subject to create a more direct sentence, and eliminate an unnecessary "that" clause.*

62. One of the major findings in the study was that Thai companies must implement global standards to increase global performance. *Two key elements of the main idea need elaboration, and a strong verb would create a more direct sentence.*

63. One of the major findings in the study was that Thai companies must improve the quality of their products to compete in the global economy. While this is a weakness, … *Second sentence includes a murky reference.*

64. Although we never actually see her in the novel, the wife of the main character … *More elaboration needed in the first clause: what does "see" mean?*

65. Christina Rossetti's poem "Goblin Market" is presented as a fairytale with a very explicit message to be drawn from its reading: there is no friend like a sister. *Write a more concise sentence that is more readable.*

66. The type of marble used and the size of the statue determined the status of the individual it represented. *Sentence includes a verb that totally flips the main point of the sentence.*

67. The type of marble used, the size of the statue, its pose, and its attire reflected the status of the individual it represented. *Group the items in*

the list along like items to more accurately reflect the importance of each item in reflecting the status.

68. The paying of salaries and other compensation was an issue that threatened the joint venture. *Complete the subject, and find a strong verb.*

69. Very few people have any type of security for their mobile devices. This means that just about everyone who owns a mobile device is susceptible to some sort of cyber-crime. *Combine the sentences to improve flow.*

70. The intent of the radicals who participated in the Boston Tea Party was to provoke a confrontation with England. *Find a more straightforward subject and a more direct verb.*

71. The ability to rescue is a key job requirement for life guards, a skill that requires more than just being a good swimmer. *Sentence includes an incomplete thought.*

72. When trying to analyze the current state of cybersecurity, we must first gather a better understanding of the extent of the threat we face. *Write a shorter, more direct sentence that is more readable.*

73. Chicago was situated near Fort Dearborn, which had previously been abandoned in 1837 by the American government because it was too far away from the concentrated population to maintain during times of conflict. *Sentence includes an unnecessary adverb, an element of the main idea that is unclear and needs elaboration, and a verb that only half-fits.*

74. A study sponsored by the Elephant Action League found that between one to three tons of ivory, fetching a monthly income of

between \$200,000 and \$600,000, passes through ports in southern Somalia every month. *Information in the participle phrase can be worked into the main clause for a shorter, more readable sentence.*

75. These individuals were committed supporters of Al-Shabaab and had trained with the terrorist organization and participated in its terrorist operations. *One idea in the sentence is implied in other ideas.*

76. A recent cyber-security study reported that millions of people are infected by malware every year. *Eliminate the careless and senseless lapse.*

77. The Austro-Hungarian Empire in July 2014 set in motion a series of steps that greatly increased the risk of a major war in Europe when it dispatched troops to the border with Serbia. Within days, Russia mobilized its Army, a step that would prompt France to do the same. Britain and Germany ... *Rearrange the first sentence to improve the flow of ideas.*

78. Chicago established itself as a center of commercial and political forces for the new frontier, and the United States as a whole. *Two adjectives do not fit with the noun they are modifying, given the context of the sentence.*

79. The country was heavily divided on the issues of women and religion, and the stress of the divisions was felt as high as the newly established parliament. *Be concise and use active voice to write a sentence with one independent clause.*

80. I wish you the best of luck in your endeavor to improve your writing, although it will take time and effort, and I know you will succeed.

"School Solutions"

1. These governments often resorted to authoritarian measures because democratic principles were not deeply established and accepted.

2. The future of cybersecurity depends largely on nations working together to raise the public's awareness of the risk and to share information on cyber threats and criminal networks.

3. The Civil War and decades of struggling for equality turned our nation into a land of enormous freedom.

4. The close proximity of countries in the Horn of Africa, including Somalia, to the Arabian Peninsula and North Africa facilitates contact and cooperation among terrorists operating in these regions.

5. France concluded an entente with Russia because the agreement would provide Paris with a major ally in a war with Germany.

6. Ngo Dign Diem was an extremely devoted (or religious) Roman Catholic, who was biased against the Buddhist majority in Vietnam.

7. Wereas previously The Beatles had used *musique concrete* only intermittently in their songs to reinforce what the music was already accomplishing lyrically and instrumentally, *musique concrète* makes up "Revolution 9" in its entirety.

8. Although the clause on unlimited liability was removed from the bill, the legislation still ...

9. Retailers prefer to sell high demand, popular brands of merchandise because ...

10. The demand for colored marbles and large monolithic columns was growing because ...

11. Fearing the spread of communism, South Korea's military seized control of the country in 1961 and did not relinquish control until 2003.

12. The narrator's conversational tone makes the story pleasant to read.

13. Edib wrote for a newspaper that was staffed with prominent writers, who worked hard to incorporate Western culture into Turkey. Few women in Turkey held such prestigious positions at that time.

14. The use of new types of stones in larger building projects demanded a change in how the quarries were administered.

15. Buddhists and Christians who served (or enlisted) in the military ...

16. Montesquieu proposed that three fundamental forms of democracy might exist—democracy, monarchy, and despotism—and he posited that each would be suitable depending on the population.

17. McAfee researchers collected 100,000 new malware samples daily in 2012, about 69 new malware samples a minute.

18. The annexation of Egypt led to an increase in the use of marble in Rome. Or: The annexation of Egypt prompted an increase in the use of marble in Rome to increase.

19. If governments and populations had valued the individual more, East Asian democracies might have obtained stability and Western-style democracy sooner.

20. China's fear that it was trapped between two powers, the Soviet Union and the United States, whose economic and political might China could not match, greatly influenced its interaction with the outside world.

21. After garment workers failed to persuade a majority of legislators to pass legislation requiring joint liability, ...

22. While the message about the bonds of sisterhood is a satisfactory story in itself, much more can be gleaned from Rossetti's "Goblin Market."

23. Although the views along Aruba's beaches are very picturesque, the beaches are remote and have few hotels. Or: Although Aruba's beaches are very picturesque, they are remote and have few hotels.

24. In the novel, the Assistant Commissioner's behavior lies in the middle of the spectrum of selfishness that is manifested in the novel.

25. The "seagull sound" in the song "Tomorrow Never Knows" is difficult to identify as Paul McCartney's laughter without knowing in advance that his laughter is in the song.

26. Rather than take a firm position against Germany's occupation of the Sudetenland, England and France acquiesced and agreed to the occupation.

27. But these peaceful demonstrations did not bring change or justice.

28. The most telling manifestation of Verloc's selfishness occurs at the end of the novel when Verloc tells Winnie about Stevie's death, and, rather than ask for forgiveness, he blames Winnie.

29. World War II officially began with the German invasion of Poland, but the origins of the war can be traced back to the decision by France and England to allow Germany to remilitarize the Rhineland. Some historians do not agree with this interpretation and attribute the origins of the war to the reparations imposed on Germany in 1918.

30. Citing the region's average annual rainfall of more than 30 inches, the farmer sought a larger land concession than the company Land-for-Sale was willing to concede.

31. Maslow's Hierarchy of Needs may help us determine whether Chris and a mall shopper have similar underlying motives that prompt one to go into the wild and another to go shopping.

32. The financial stability and positive outlook for CAT is mainly due to the company's goals to provide industry-leading construction equipment and ever-expanding customer support.

33. Martial law in Taiwan and South Korea ended in the late 1980s when a broadly supported movement of "people power" pushed for liberalization and reform.

34. First sentence needs elaboration on who the researchers are and what they are researching.

35. When academic concepts are taught to English language learners in their native language, …

36. The extraction of marble requires tools and methods that are different from those used in the extraction of other stones, such as limestone.

37. Shaarawi insisted that her education be continued even as she was told that it was unnecessary for her station in life. She wrote that "being a female became a barrier between me and the freedom for which I yearned," a reference to the life-long opposition she encountered to continuing her education.

38. While improved labor conditions and higher wages are necessary to prevent employee abuse, over regulation of private companies will reduce their profitability.

39. The Diem government did not allow Buddhists monks to show their love for their beliefs, prompting some of them to set themselves on fire.

40. Al Shabaab slowly transformed itself from an insurgency focused only on national goals to the most powerful Jihadi organization in the region.

41. The sculptor in ancient times had to break down the process of creating a statue into a set of clearly defined, ordered steps.

42. The company's most important acquisition was the purchase of a patent that provided increased traction and stability for construction equipment.

43. While the Business and Competitive Analysis textbook does not specifically discuss (or address) strategy for global companies, many of its frameworks and models would benefit Thai technology firms.

44. The structure of beams and posts that can be seen from inside the building is a complex work of engineering.

45. Without retail price maintenance agreements, manufacturers would have no control over the price of their products or how much retailers might discount the selling price.

46. A narrator's chief task is to bridge the gap between the reader and the story by providing details about the time, place, setting, and characters.

47. When examining the main characters in the plot …

48. CAT's products also were used in other historically significant construction projects, such as the Hoover Dam and the English Channel.

49. A machine does not experience happiness when it completes an assigned task.

50. The blast radius [or destructive zone] of the H-bombs developed in the 1950s—some of which were 2 megaton devices—extended out to 20 miles.

51. My drawings are not to be interpreted after a single look but to be pondered and considered over time.

52. The discovery of effective medicines and the development of new medical technologies have increased life expectancy in America to about 77 years for men and 82 years for women.

53. The retail industry must comply with fair competition regulations, such as the antitrust laws, while still earning a profit and remaining competitive.

54. The occupation of foreign lands by Western powers is fueling religious terrorism today, making the United States homeland, as well as its interests abroad, a focus for terrorists.

55. Portraits in the main hall of Chew's niece Margret Oswald and his nephew Joseph Turner highlight his strong relationship with his family.

56. While other artists created allegorical and traditional landscape paintings that had little or no political significance, Goya directly confronted his time with paintings that exuded political commentary.

57. During my two-year stay in Greece, I visited the islands of Crete, Euboea, Cephalonia, Lesbos, Chios, Rhodes, Corfu, and Samos.

58. The vast quantity of marble used throughout the empire attests (or "is evidence of") to its extensive influence on both Roman art and architecture.

59. The similarities between Rossetti's poem and the Bible should be interpreted more as symbols and allusions than as bits and pieces of an overarching Bible allegory.

60. Terrorist groups exploit the social and economic inequalities that are common in the region to recruit new terrorists and cultivate sympathizers.

61. Hackers can use any of several methods to attack your device depending on what it is they are trying to accomplish.

62. The study concluded that Thai companies must improve the quality of their products to compete in the global economy.

63. The study concluded that Thai companies must improve the quality of their products to compete in the global economy. While poor product quality is a weakness, ...

64. Although the wife of the main character only appears in the novel as a subject of conversation and others' thoughts, she ...

65. Christina Rossetti's poem Goblin Market is presented as a fairytale with a very explicit message: there is no friend like a sister.

66. The type of marble used and the size of the statue reflected the status of the individual it represented.

67. The type of marble used and the statute's size, pose, and attire reflected the status of the individual it represented.

68. Disagreement over the paying of salaries and other compensation threatened the joint venture.

69. Very few people have any type of security for their mobile devices, making just about anyone who owns a mobile device susceptible to some sort of cyber-crime.

70. The radicals who participated in the Boston Tea Party wanted to provoke a confrontation with England.

71. The ability to rescue swimmers who are in distress and panicking is a key job requirement for life guards and a skill that requires more than just being a good swimmer.

72. When analyzing the current state of cybersecurity, we must first understand the extent of the threat we face.

73. Chicago was situated near Fort Dearborn, which was abandoned by the American government in 1837 because it was too far away from the major population centers to defend during times of conflict.

74. A study sponsored by the Elephant Action League found that between one to three tons of ivory, worth between $200,000 and $600,000, passes through ports in southern Somalia every month.

75. These individuals had trained with Al-Shabaab and participated in its terrorist operations.

76. A recent cyber-security study reported that millions of computers are infected by malware every year.

77. The Austro-Hungarian Empire in July 2014 dispatched troops to its border with Serbia, setting in motion a series of steps that greatly increased the risk of a major war in Europe. Within days, Russia mobilized its Army, a step that would prompt France to do the same. Britain and Germany ...

78. Chicago established itself as a center of commercial and political power for the new frontier, and the United States as a whole.

79. The issues of women and religion deeply divided and stressed the country, including the newly established parliament.

80. I wish you the best of luck in your endeavor to improve your writing. It will take time and effort, but I know you will succeed.

Notes

Notes

Notes

Notes

CPSIA information can be obtained at www.ICGtesting.com
Printed in the USA
LVOW06s1822120815

449845LV00020B/1067/P